MW01116101

Table of Contents

CHAPTER NINE: EVALUATING AND IMPROVING PROGRAMS AND SERVICES 197

CHAPTER TEN: UNDERSTANDING LEGAL AND RISK 219

CHAPTER ELEVEN: LEVERAGING TECHNOLOGY 247

CHAPTER TWELVE: COMMUNICATING YOUR STORY AND BRAND .. 279

Disclaimer & Copyright

writing from the author or publisher, except by a reviewer who may quote brief passages in a review.

Foreword

Bob Harris, CAE

When a nonprofit organization asks for "help," it is always an honor to be invited inside. Many seek the counsel of an expert who will guide them to increase performance and to achieve their mission.

Bill Pawlucy, CAE, has been invited into thousands of associations, chambers of commerce, and other nonprofits. Nearly every week he shares the smartest practices, the newest resources, and a determination for the organization to excel.

In *The Essential Handbook for Nonprofit Leaders*, he outlines the possibilities for nonprofits, which exceed more than 1.5 million organizations in the USA. He is invited in to untangle difficult situations, elevate boards, and to set a powerful and strategic course of action.

Whether in the book or inside the association, he does not hold back his passion for success. Keep *The Essential Handbook for Nonprofit Leaders* on the staff bookshelf and display it on the board table. You'll find this to be the "bible" for nonprofits in America.

Dedication

This book is dedicated to my wife Dana, who has always been my rock and my source of unwavering love and support. You consistently challenge me to reach beyond my own limits and strive for greatness. Your unwavering belief in me has been a driving force in my journey to success. Thank you for pushing me to be the best version of myself.

To my two amazing sons, Nicholas and Noah, who are the source of endless joy and positivity in my life. Your inquisitive minds and sharp intellects never cease to amaze me and serve as a constant source of inspiration.

To my daughters, Emma and Eloise, who are growing into strong, confident young women. Your courage and resilience fill me with pride and I can't wait to see all the amazing things you will accomplish in the future.

And finally, to Bob Harris, CAE, my mentor and dear friend, who is not only part of the family but an integral part of this journey. Your wisdom, guidance, and unwavering belief in me have been invaluable.

To all of you, I am eternally grateful. This book is for you.

Chapter One: The Impact of America's Nonprofits

Nonprofits play a critical role in the fabric of American society, contributing to the well-being of communities, the advancement of important causes, professional and business development, and the creation of meaningful opportunities for individuals to make a positive impact. From small local organizations to large national associations, nonprofits are an integral part of the American landscape, impacting every aspect of our lives in meaningful ways.

This chapter examines the impact that nonprofits have on American society, analyzing their extent of influence, the challenges they face, and the opportunities they provide. By exploring these aspects, readers will gain a comprehensive understanding of the significance of nonprofits and their indispensable role in strengthening our communities and nation.

Reach of Nonprofits in America

There are over 1.5 million registered nonprofits in the United States, covering a vast array of causes, from healthcare and human services, to education, the arts, the trades, business trades, and the environment.

In 2019, these organizations received over $450 billion in contributions, and employed over 12 million people. The impact of this work is felt by millions of individuals and communities across the country, making nonprofits an essential part of the American experience.

Influence of Nonprofits

Nonprofit charities and membership associations both play crucial roles in American society, but their contributions differ in significant ways. Nonprofit charities provide essential services to those in need, such as food and shelter for the homeless, support for families dealing with illnesses, and education and job training for underprivileged communities. On the other hand, nonprofit membership associations elevate professionals and drive growth in various industries by offering education, networking opportunities, and professional development resources.

Membership associations have a significant impact in helping professionals enhance their skills, stay current on industry trends, and build their careers. By providing a platform for members to connect and collaborate, membership associations also foster innovation and drive growth in various industries, creating new job opportunities and promoting economic development.

Both nonprofit charities and membership associations serve as a voice for those who may not have one, advocating for change, bridging the gap between the public and government, and making a considerable impact on various aspects of our lives. Through their advocacy work, they help marginalized communities to be heard and their needs addressed. Nonprofit charities provide disaster relief services and defend individual rights and liberties, while membership associations promote economic development, advocate for favorable policies, and provide networking and professional development opportunities for their members.

Nonprofit organizations span a broad spectrum of professional business and trade associations that play a critical role in commerce across the United States. These membership associations offer a range of services and benefits to their members, such as networking opportunities, professional development resources, and advocacy on behalf of their respective industries. Through their work, nonprofit membership associations contribute to the growth and success of countless businesses and professionals, elevating their skills and promoting their interests.

In short, nonprofits have an immense influence on society, shaping our communities and our nation in meaningful ways. When driving important conversations, providing critical services, or bridging the gap between government and the public, nonprofits are an essential part of the American experience, making a positive impact every day.

Challenges Facing Nonprofits

Despite their importance and impact, nonprofits face a number of challenges in their work. These challenges include:

- **Funding:** Nonprofits rely on member dues, event revenues, sponsorships, contributions, and grants to support their work, and securing this funding can be a major challenge, particularly in an uncertain economic environment.

- **Competition:** With so many nonprofits vying for attention and resources, it can be difficult for organizations to stand out and gain the recognition and support they need to succeed.

- **Regulation:** Nonprofits must navigate a complex web of regulations, from tax laws to charitable giving rules, in order to operate effectively and maintain their status.

- **Leadership:** Nonprofits require strong, visionary leadership in order to achieve their goals and make a lasting impact. Finding and developing this leadership can be a challenge, especially for smaller organizations.

- **Collaboration:** Nonprofits often work in silos, lacking the partnerships and collaborations that could allow them to maximize their impact. This should be a critical area in a nonprofit's strategic plan.

IRS Classifications of Nonprofits

The tax code provides various tax classifications (there are 29!) for nonprofits, each with their own specific set of rules and regulations. Some of the most common tax classifications for nonprofits include:

- **501(c)(3) Organizations:** These organizations are considered charitable organizations and are eligible for tax-exempt status. They also can be membership organizations as well. They are generally focused on providing charitable services to the general public. Donations made to these organizations are tax-deductible for donors. However, 501(c)(3) organizations are restricted from engaging in political activities, including lobbying and electioneering.

- **501(c)(4) Organizations:** These organizations are social welfare organizations and are also eligible for tax-exempt status. They are allowed to engage in limited political activities, including lobbying and electioneering, as long as these activities are not the primary purpose of the organization. Donations made to these organizations are not tax-deductible for donors.

- **501(c)(5) Organizations:** These organizations are labor, agricultural, and horticultural organizations and are eligible for tax-exempt status. They are allowed to engage in lobbying and political activities, but these activities must be directly related to their primary purpose of promoting the interests of their members. Donations made to these organizations are not tax-deductible for donors.

- **501(c)(6) Organizations:** These organizations are trade associations, professional organizations, or business leagues, and are eligible for tax-exempt status. They are allowed to engage in unlimited lobbying and political activities, as long as these activities are directly related to promoting the common interests of their members. Donations made to these organizations are not tax-deductible for donors.

In summary, the various tax classifications of nonprofits have different rules and regulations around lobbying and political activities. While some organizations (such as 501(c)(3) organizations) are restricted from engaging in these activities, others (such as 501(c)(4), 501(c)(5), and 501(c)(6) organizations) are allowed to engage in limited or unlimited lobbying and political activities, depending on their primary purpose and the nature of their activities.

As per the Internal Revenue Service, there are a total of 29 501(c) classifications. It is difficult to determine the exact number of organizations under each of those tax classifications, as this information is constantly changing. However, as of 2021, the IRS reports that there are over 1.5 million tax-exempt organizations in the United States, with the majority of these being classified as 501(c)(3) organizations.

Among the other tax classifications, 501(c)(4) organizations are the second largest group, followed by 501(c)(6) organizations. The number of organizations under each classification may vary based on various factors, such as changes in the tax code and in the regulatory environment.

It is important to note that the number of organizations under each tax classification does not necessarily reflect their relative size or influence. Organizations under each classification can range from small local organizations to large national organizations with significant resources and impact.

In this book, our primary focus will be on 501(c)(3) and 501(c)(6) organizations, as these are the most commonly utilized and well-known classifications and exhibit a significant number of differences between them.

The difference between a 501(c)(3) and a 501(c)(6) organization lies in the nature of their activities and the tax benefits they are eligible for.

501(c)(3) organizations are considered charitable organizations and are eligible for tax-exempt status. This means that they do not have to pay taxes on the income they generate from their operations. Additionally, contributions made to these organizations are tax-deductible for donors. Some common examples of 501(c)(3) organizations include charities, religious organizations, educational institutions, and scientific research organizations.

It is important to also make the distinction that not all 501(c)(3) organizations are foundations, but many are membership associations. A 501(c)(3) organization can be a membership organization if it provides membership benefits such as access to exclusive events, educational resources, or discounts to its members.

However, it is important for the 501(c)(3) organization to maintain its tax-exempt status by following the guidelines set forth by the Internal Revenue Service (IRS). This means that membership dues cannot be the primary source of funding for the organization, and any lobbying activities must be limited. The organization must also ensure that its membership activities are consistent with its mission and purpose as a tax-exempt organization. To maintain its tax-exempt status, the 501(c)(3) membership organization should seek the guidance of an attorney or accountant who specializes in nonprofit law.

On the other hand, 501(c)(6) organizations are considered trade associations, professional organizations, or business leagues. They are also eligible for tax-exempt status, but their activities are focused on promoting the common interests of their members, rather than on providing charitable services to the general public. Donations made to these organizations are not tax-deductible for the donors. Some common examples of 501(c)(6) organizations include chambers of commerce, trade organizations, professional societies, and real estate boards.

Lobbying Differences

First, let's start with the lobbying differences. *Lobbying* refers to the attempt to influence legislation or government action. Nonprofits are allowed to engage in lobbying activities, but the extent to which they can do so is determined by their tax classification.

501(c)(3) organizations are generally restricted from lobbying activities. According to IRS regulations, lobbying by these organizations must be limited and not a "substantial part" of their activities. If a 501(c)(3) organization engages in too much lobbying, it risks losing its tax-exempt status.

On the other hand, other tax classifications, such as 501(c)(4), 501(c)(5), and 501(c)(6) organizations, are generally allowed to engage in unlimited lobbying activities as long as these activities are related to their primary purpose. For example, a 501(c)(4) organization can engage in unlimited lobbying as long as its primary purpose is promoting social welfare, while a 501(c)(6) organization can engage in unlimited lobbying as long as its primary purpose is promoting the common interests of its members.

It is important to note that while nonprofits are allowed to engage in lobbying activities, they must still comply with all relevant regulations, including disclosure requirements and limits on campaign contributions. Additionally, they must ensure that their lobbying activities do not conflict with their tax-exempt status or compromise their mission.

Since 501(c)(3) organizations are generally restricted from lobbying activities, they can file a Form 5768. The IRS Form 5768 is a form used by 501(c)(3) organizations to make an election under the Internal Revenue Code section 501(h) to be subject to an expenditure test for lobbying activities. Through this election, a 501(c)(3) organization can opt to be subject to an expenditure test for lobbying, which allows it to spend a certain amount of its resources on lobbying activities each year. The expenditure limit is calculated based on a percentage of the organization's total exempt purpose expenses and varies based on the size of the organization.

Making this election can provide a 501(c)(3) organization with greater flexibility to engage in lobbying activities while still maintaining its tax-exempt status. However, it is important to note that the election is a significant commitment and that the organization must carefully track its lobbying expenses and comply with all relevant regulations. Additionally, the election can have implications for the organization's donors and its lobbying activities may be subject to greater scrutiny.

More Than Just Foundations and Charities

As previously mentioned, it's worth noting again that nonprofit entities are not restricted to foundations and philanthropic organizations only. They can also include membership-based organizations that aim to facilitate growth within a specific profession or industry. This encompasses a diverse range of entities including business, trade, healthcare, and other types of membership associations that exist to serve their members. This highlights the diversity and versatility of the nonprofit sector and its ability to serve a wide range of needs and causes.

For example, business associations, such as chambers of commerce, trade organizations, and professional associations, can be organized as nonprofits. Business associations play a vital role in bringing together businesses and trades of similar types and sizes to advocate for their interests, promote their industries, and provide support and resources to their members. They serve as a voice for their constituents and help to shape the policies, regulations, and standards that impact their respective industries and professions.

Healthcare organizations, such as profession-related associations, hospitals, health clinics, and patient advocacy groups are another example of nonprofits that are not typically thought of as foundations or philanthropic organizations. These organizations may provide healthcare services, conduct research, provide resources, educate their members, and advocate for better health policies and programs.

Similarly, other types of nonprofits, such as cultural organizations, environmental groups, and advocacy organizations, also play a significant role in American society and have a diverse range of missions and activities.

It is important to understand that while the missions and activities of nonprofits may vary widely, they all share a common goal of serving the public interest and making a positive impact on society. Whether they are foundations, philanthropic organizations, business associations, healthcare organizations, or other types of nonprofits, nonprofits play a vital role

in shaping the fabric of American society and
addressing the challenges of our time.

Opportunities for Nonprofits

Nonprofit organizations play a critical role in the
fabric of our society, offering valuable services,
fostering community engagement, and making a
meaningful impact on the lives of millions of people.
Compared to for-profit entities, nonprofits possess
unique attributes that make them especially well-
suited to addressing pressing societal needs and
improving the world around us. From driving
innovation and progress to serving as a bridge
between government and the public, nonprofits offer
a wide range of benefits and opportunities for
individuals, communities, and the nation as a whole.

The following list highlights just a few of the ways in
which nonprofits are well-positioned to achieve their
goals and make a positive difference in the world:

- **Innovation:** Nonprofits have the ability to
  pursue unconventional ideas and approaches
  that are not limited by the pressure to generate

profit, allowing them to drive forward-thinking solutions and progress.

- **Community engagement:** As a mediator between the government and the public, nonprofits can cultivate relationships and foster collaboration between communities, ultimately leading to greater social cohesion and cooperation.

- **Impact:** By dedicating their efforts solely to advancing social good, nonprofits have the ability to reach those in need and make a significant impact on the lives of many.

- **Elevation:** Through offering educational opportunities, certification programs, and professional development resources to their members, nonprofits play a vital role in uplifting professions and promoting career growth.

The impact of America's nonprofits cannot be overstated. These organizations play a critical role in our communities and our nation, serving as a voice for the voiceless, driving progress and change, and providing critical services.

Agility

The agility of nonprofits is what sets them apart and makes them a vital force in our society. Like a skilled gymnast, nonprofits must be able to contort and pivot in response to the ever-changing landscape of social needs and community demands. They must be nimble in their approach, fluid in their thinking, and innovative in their solutions. It is this ability to adapt and respond that makes nonprofits so critical in driving progress and impacting lives in meaningful ways. Ensuring that nonprofits remain nimble, therefore, should be a top priority for all those who care about the future of our communities and the world at large.

This book will extensively cover various strategies that can help ensure the adaptability and flexibility of nonprofit organizations in achieving their goals and mission. These strategies include:

- Regularly evaluating the organization's goals and strategies to ensure they are aligned with the current needs of stakeholders.

- Fostering a culture of innovation and experimentation to encourage staff and volunteers to generate new ideas and approaches to challenges.
- Promoting collaboration and communication among team members, board members, and stakeholders to facilitate collective problem-solving and decision-making.
- Maintaining a flexible organizational structure that can respond quickly to environmental changes and seize new opportunities.
- Leveraging technology and digital tools to streamline operations and improve efficiency.
- Encouraging a culture of continuous learning and development to help staff and volunteers enhance their skills and knowledge.

By following these steps, nonprofits can ensure that they remain nimble, adaptive, and able to meet the changing needs of their stakeholders.

Chapter Two: Framing Your Mission

A nonprofit's mission statement is more than just a few words on a piece of paper or a website—it's the foundation upon which everything else is built. It's a concise and clear declaration of purpose that captures the essence of why the organization exists and what it hopes to achieve. A powerful mission statement can inspire and guide an organization, as well as attract support from stakeholders such as donors, volunteers, and partners.

The mission statement is the foundation of a nonprofit's identity and can shape the organization's culture, direction, and impact. It helps to define what the organization stands for, what it seeks to achieve, and how it will measure success. This, in turn, helps to create a shared sense of purpose among the organization's leaders, staff, volunteers, and stakeholders, making it easier for everyone to work together towards a common goal.

For stakeholders, the mission statement provides a clear understanding of what the organization does and why it's important. It can be a powerful tool for attracting and retaining members and supporters, whether that's through donations, volunteer hours, or partnerships. By articulating its mission clearly, an organization can build trust and credibility, and demonstrate its commitment to making a meaningful difference in the world and the industries it serves.

Creating a well-crafted and impactful mission statement is an essential step in establishing a clear and effective organizational purpose. Here are some key considerations when framing your mission statement:

- **Be concise:** A mission statement should be brief and to the point, typically no more than a few sentences.
- **Be clear:** A mission statement should clearly articulate the organization's purpose and, specifically, why it exists.
- **Be inspiring:** A mission statement should be inspiring and motivate others to get involved and support the organization's cause.
- **Reflect your values:** A mission statement should reflect the values and beliefs of the organization and the people it serves.

- **Focus on impact:** A mission statement should focus on the impact the organization hopes to achieve and the difference it wants to make in the world.
- **Consider your audience:** A mission statement should be written in language that is easily understood by your target audience, whether they are members, donors, volunteers, staff, or other key stakeholders.

By following these guidelines, an organization can frame its mission statement in a way that is clear, concise, and inspiring, and that reflects the values and goals of the organization. In short, a nonprofit's mission statement is a critical component of its success.

A well-crafted mission statement serves as the beacon for a nonprofit, illuminating the path towards creating meaningful change in the world. Whether it's a member, volunteer, donor, staff, or just someone who shares a passion for the organization's cause, a strong mission statement helps articulate the positive impact the organization aims to bring about.

Steps In Developing a Mission

As demonstrated, a mission statement is your purpose, or the "why" behind the organization's existence. Developing a mission statement is a critical process for any nonprofit organization, as it lays the foundation for the organization's direction, strategy, and impact.

Here are some surefire steps to take when developing a mission statement:

- **Gather information:** Before writing a mission statement, it's important to gather information about the organization's history, values, goals, and the needs of the members and communities it serves. This can be achieved through research, surveys, focus groups, and conversations with stakeholders.
- **Define the purpose:** Clearly define the organization's purpose, including what it does and why it's important. Consider what sets the organization apart from others and what unique value it brings to its stakeholders.

- **Engage stakeholders:** Involve staff, volunteers, board members, and other stakeholders in the process of developing the mission statement. Seek input and feedback to ensure that the statement accurately reflects the collective vision and values of the organization.

- **Make it actionable:** The mission statement should be more than just words on paper. It should be a call to action that inspires the organization to take concrete steps towards achieving its goals.

- **Write and revise:** Use the information gathered and the input of stakeholders to craft a clear, concise, and inspiring mission statement. Be sure to make revisions as needed to ensure that the statement accurately reflects the organization's goals and objectives.

- **Test and refine:** Once the mission statement has been written, test it to ensure that it is clear, concise, and inspiring. Refine the statement as necessary to ensure that it accurately reflects the organization's purpose and goals.

- **Communicate the mission:** Once the mission statement has been developed, be sure to communicate it widely to stakeholders, including staff, volunteers, donors, and partners. Use the statement to guide decision-making and ensure that everyone is working towards a common goal.

Great Mission Statement Examples

These mission statements are clear, concise, and reflect each of these organizations' reason for existence. They are inspiring and motivate members and stakeholders to be part of the organization's efforts to advance the interests of the cause, profession, or industry. Use them as models of excellence when developing the organization's mission.

- **Doctors Without Borders:** "To provide medical assistance to people affected by conflict, epidemics, disasters, or exclusion from health care."
- **National Retail Federation:** "To deliver value and drive growth for retailers and the industry."

- **American Red Cross:** "The American Red Cross prevents and alleviates human suffering in the face of emergencies by mobilizing the power of volunteers and the generosity of donors."

- **National Federation of Independent Business:** "To promote and protect the right of our members to own, operate, and grow their businesses."

- **The Nature Conservancy:** "To conserve the lands and waters on which all life depends."

- **National Association of Home Builders:** " To protect the American Dream of housing opportunities for all, while working to achieve professional success for its members who build communities, create jobs and strengthen our economy."

- **World Wildlife Fund:** "To leverage sound science to conserve nature and reduce the most pressing threats to the diversity of life on Earth."

- **Oxfam America:** "We fight inequality to end poverty and injustice."

- **United Way Worldwide:** "To improve lives by mobilizing the caring power of communities around the world to advance the common good."

These mission statements are effective because they are both memorable and clearly communicate the purpose of each organization. They are concise, easy to understand, and communicate the positive impact the organization aims to make in its respective field. These statements provide a clear direction for the organization and its stakeholders and inspire them to work towards a common goal. Additionally, they help build trust and credibility with members, donors, volunteers, and other stakeholders, as they demonstrate the organization's commitment to its mission and the positive change it is striving to achieve.

Maintaining the Mission's Visibility and Relevance

As we delve into the intricacies of mission statements, it becomes clear that having one is simply not enough. The true test of an organization's commitment to its mission lies in how well it keeps that mission at the forefront of all its actions and decisions.

Think of it this way: A mission statement is like a North Star, guiding an organization towards its ultimate destination. But it's not enough to simply know where you're going—you must continually course-correct to ensure that you remain on track.

So, how can organizations keep their mission statement front and center in everything they do?

First, it's essential to make the mission statement part of the organizational culture. It should be included in staff training, board meetings, messaging, and day-to-day decision-making processes. This will ensure that everyone within the organization is aware of the mission and is working towards it.

Second, it's crucial to measure progress against the mission. Regularly evaluating progress will provide insight into whether the organization is on track and, if not, what changes need to be made.

Third, the mission statement must be regularly reviewed and updated if necessary. As the organization evolves, its mission may change, and it's essential to ensure that the mission statement reflects this.

Finally, the mission statement should be communicated externally. Share it with stakeholders, including members, donors, supporters, and the wider community. This will help to build a sense of shared purpose and strengthen support for the organization's work.

Keeping a mission statement front and center requires a holistic approach that encompasses culture, measurement, review, and communication. By doing so, organizations can ensure that they remain true to their purpose and make a lasting impact in the world.

Return on Mission

Return on investment (ROI) is a common metric used to measure the financial performance of businesses. It's calculated by dividing the profit generated by an investment by the amount of money invested.

While ROI is a useful metric for evaluating financial performance, it has limitations when it comes to measuring the impact of nonprofits. One major limitation is that it fails to account for non-monetary outcomes. Many nonprofits exist to address social problems, business challenges, and promote public good, which may not have an immediate or direct financial return. For example, an organization working to reduce crime in a community may not see an immediate financial return, but the social benefits of a safer community are invaluable.

Another issue is that ROI does not take into account the broader social and environmental impact of an organization's work. For example, an organization working to promote sustainability may not have a high financial return, but their work has a positive impact on the environment, which cannot be measured in financial terms.

Finally, ROI focuses on short-term results and may not reflect the long-term impact of an organization's work. For example, an organization working to build the workforce in the restaurant space may not see a direct financial return for several years, but their efforts will pay off in the long run by increasing the workforce.

While ROI is a useful metric for evaluating financial performance, it is not enough to fully capture the impact of nonprofits. To truly measure the impact of their work, nonprofits must also consider non-monetary outcomes, broader social and environmental impact, and long-term results. That is where return on mission (ROM) comes into play.

Our concept of ROM is one that has become increasingly relevant in today's nonprofit landscape and complements ROI in many ways. In a world where resources are finite and competition for funding is fierce, organizations must demonstrate their impact and prove that they are making a meaningful difference.

Imagine this: An organization has a mission to end homelessness. They work tirelessly to provide housing, support services, and job training to those in need. But how do they know if their efforts are having the desired effect?

This is where return on mission comes in. It's the idea that organizations should measure the impact they're having against their mission, much in the same way that businesses measure their financial return on investment. By doing so, organizations can assess their effectiveness, identify areas for improvement, and ultimately demonstrate their value to members, funders, supporters, and the communities they serve.

It's important to note that return on mission is not a one-size-fits-all concept. The metrics used to measure impact will vary depending on the organization's mission, the population and members they serve, and the outcomes they seek to achieve.

So, how can organizations measure their return on mission? There are a variety of tools and frameworks available, including logic models, outcome tracking systems, and impact assessments. The key is to choose the right approach for your organization and use it to track progress, analyze data, and make informed decisions that drive impact.

Return on mission is a powerful concept that can help organizations maximize their impact, demonstrate their value, and secure the funding and support they need to continue their vital work. By embracing this concept and regularly measuring their impact, nonprofits can ensure that they are making a real difference in the world and for their key stakeholders.

Combining ROI and ROM

Using both ROM and ROI is like looking at a picture from two different angles. ROI provides a snapshot of the financial health of an organization, but fails to take into account the wider impact of the nonprofit's work. ROM, on the other hand, seeks to measure the impact of the nonprofit's work in terms of its ability to achieve its mission. By looking at both metrics, nonprofits are able to gain a more complete picture of their impact and effectiveness.

Let's take a look at a hypothetical business membership association as an example. The organization's mission is to support and promote the growth of small businesses in the local community.

Using the metric of ROI, the organization will look at the revenue generated from sources such as membership fees, sponsorships, and events. For example, the organization might calculate the total cost of running events, such as networking events and conferences, and compare it to the revenue generated from ticket sales. If the revenue generated is higher than the cost of running the events, the organization might see this as a positive ROI.

However, if we take a look at the same organization through the lens of ROM, we can consider the impact the organization is having on the local business community. This might involve looking at the number of businesses that have joined the organization, the number of businesses that have benefited from the organization's services and events, and the overall impact that the organization experienced on the local business community.

For example, let's say the organization has 500 members, and the events and services it offers have helped those members generate an additional $10 million in revenue. In this case, the ROM would be considered very high, as the organization's work has directly impacted the financial success of its members.

By combining both metrics, the organization is able to gain a more comprehensive understanding of its impact and effectiveness as well as ensuring that its efforts are aligned with its mission and focused on achieving its goals. For example, it can see that its events are generating revenue, but also understand the impact that those events are having on its members and the local business community. This information can then be used to make informed decisions about future events and initiatives, ensuring that the organization's work is aligned with its mission and focused on achieving its goals.

Importance of Updating a Mission Statement

Revisiting and refreshing a mission statement is crucial in maintaining its relevance and alignment with the organization's goals and objectives. It's essential to regularly evaluate the impact and effectiveness of the mission statement and make any necessary modifications to keep it in line with the evolving needs and priorities of the organization. By doing this, leaders ensure that the mission statement remains a guiding force in decision-making and resource allocation, helping to steer the organization towards continued success and impact.

Failure to keep the mission statement current can lead to disconnect and confusion, hindering the organization's ability to achieve its goals and serve its stakeholders effectively.

To ensure the relevance and alignment of the mission statement with the organization's goals and objectives, it is important to review and update it regularly. The following steps can help to keep the mission statement fresh:

1. **Assess the current state of the organization**: Evaluate the changes that have taken place within the organization and determine whether the mission statement accurately reflects the current priorities and objectives.
2. **Gather input from stakeholders**: Ask for feedback from members, volunteers, staff, and other stakeholders to get their perspectives on the mission statement and how it aligns with their expectations and goals.
3. **Evaluate the language**: Ensure that the mission statement is written in clear, concise language that can be easily understood by everyone in the organization. Consider whether any

changes or updates need to be made to better reflect the organization's goals and objectives.

4. **Consider the organization's future**: Consider whether the mission statement accurately reflects the plans and aspirations for the future of the organization.

5. **Update the statement**: Revise the mission statement as needed to ensure it remains relevant and in line with the organization's goals and objectives.

6. **Communicate the update**: Share the updated mission statement with stakeholders to ensure everyone is aware of the changes and understands the organization's priorities and objectives.

By following these steps, you can keep your mission statement fresh and ensure it continues to guide your decision-making and resource allocation for years to come.

Chapter Three: Building a Board of Directors

The success of a nonprofit organization often rests on the shoulders of its board of directors. A strong board provides crucial governance, strategic planning, and financial oversight, while also serving as ambassadors to its members and the community and supporting its growth efforts.

But building such a board requires intentional effort and a clear understanding of the roles and responsibilities of each member. Here are some key topics to consider when building a strong board of directors.

Defining Roles and Responsibilities

In the world of nonprofits, the importance of a well-defined board of directors cannot be overstated. Just as a building's foundation provides structure and support, a strong board is the backbone of any successful organization. Defining the roles and responsibilities of board members is a critical step in ensuring that your organization is moving in the right direction.

A clear understanding of what is expected of each board member is vital for the smooth operation of the organization. Each individual should have a clear sense of their personal responsibilities, as well as a grasp of the overall duties of the board. This clarity ensures that each member is fully engaged and that the board as a whole is working together efficiently and effectively.

Additionally, a well-defined set of responsibilities helps to ensure that board members are held accountable for their actions. This accountability not only protects the organization, but it also strengthens the board's commitment to the mission and provides a clear roadmap for decision-making and resource allocation.

Board responsibilities can vary depending on the organization and sector, but generally they include:

- Overseeing the overall direction and strategy of the organization.

- Approving the annual budget and monitoring the financial health of the organization.

- Ensuring legal and ethical compliance, including following regulations and laws relevant to the organization.

- Hiring and evaluating the performance of the CEO or executive director.

- Fostering a strong culture of governance and collaboration within the board.

- Building relationships with stakeholders, including members, donors, partners, and the wider community.

- Ensuring the organization's mission is being fulfilled and the impact is being measured.

- Approving major initiatives, programs, and investments.

- Representing the organization and promoting its mission to its members and the wider community.

- Ensuring the organization has adequate resources, including finances and personnel, to achieve its goals.

A well-defined set of roles and responsibilities is essential to building a strong and effective board of directors. It provides clarity and direction, creates accountability, and strengthens the overall health of the organization. By paying attention to this important aspect of board development, nonprofits can build a foundation that will sustain them for years to come.

As stewards of the organization, the Board is responsible for providing strategic leadership, selectively implementing through resource development, and protecting through oversight. On the other hand, the Chief Executive is responsible for implementing an efficient and effective path forward, within boundaries, toward the Strategic Vision in ways that are responsive to stakeholders. Together, they steer the organization towards success by governing with purpose and accountability.

Board Fiduciary Responsibilities

Let us delve into the concept of fiduciary duties of a board of directors. As the guardians of an organization, the board of directors holds a unique position of trust, where they are responsible for overseeing the operations of the nonprofit and ensuring that it fulfills its mission.

This responsibility is not just a moral obligation, but a legal one as well. The board has a fiduciary duty to act in the best interest of the organization, which means making decisions that are in line with its mission, values, and goals.

Fiduciary duties can be broken down into three key components: duty of care, duty of loyalty, and duty of obedience.

- **Duty of Care:** The duty of care requires board members to exercise due diligence in decision-making and be informed about the issues affecting the organization.
- **Duty of Loyalty:** The duty of loyalty requires board members to put the organization's interests ahead of their own and avoid conflicts of interest.
- **Duty of Obedience:** The duty of obedience requires the board to abide by the laws and

regulations governing the organization, as well as its bylaws and mission statement.

To fulfill these fiduciary duties, the board must be informed, engaged, and accountable. This means regularly reviewing and updating policies, seeking out relevant information, and actively participating in board meetings, regular board training, and discussions. By doing so, the board can help ensure that the organization is on a solid footing and that its mission is being carried out effectively.

In short, the fiduciary duties of a board of directors are essential to the success of a nonprofit. They ensure that the organization operates in an ethical and transparent manner, and that its mission is being fulfilled in the best possible way.

Authority to Govern as a Trustee

The authority to govern a nonprofit organization stems from two critical sources. First, the state incorporation status of the organization grants it the authority to operate as a state corporation. Second, the federal status, overseen by the Department of the

Treasury and the Internal Revenue Service (IRS), provides exemption from federal income tax.

It is important to note that as an incorporated entity, each board member is considered a trustee of the state corporation. Every board member is entrusted with the responsibility of overseeing and managing the affairs of the nonprofit corporation on behalf of its stakeholders. This significant role requires the board to act in the best interests of the organization while upholding fiduciary duties.

Fulfilling fiduciary responsibilities requires every individual board member to act with care, loyalty, and obedience. This requires the board to make informed decisions, manage the organization's resources effectively, and avoid conflicts of interest. Furthermore, as trustees, there is accountability to both state and federal laws and regulations.

It is crucial to recognize that nonprofit corporations are subject to strict legal and regulatory requirements, including tax laws, employment laws, and reporting obligations. Failure to comply with these laws may result in the loss of the organization's tax-exempt status, legal liability, and damage to the organization's reputation.

Therefore, the role as a trustee must be taken seriously and ensure that the board is always acting in the best interests of the organization while complying with all applicable laws and regulations. This includes seeking legal and financial advice when necessary, participating in ongoing training and development, and conducting regular reviews of the organization's compliance with applicable laws and regulations.

Recruiting the Right People

The search for the ideal board member is a critical step for any nonprofit organization seeking to establish a strong and effective governance structure. Finding the right individuals to serve on the board requires careful consideration and a thorough understanding of the organization's goals and needs and how that aligns with its strategic plan.

Passion is an essential trait that should be sought after when searching for ideal board members. Individuals who are passionate about the organization's mission and purpose are more likely to be engaged and committed to their role as board members. They are willing to put in the time and effort necessary to help the organization achieve its objectives.

At the same time, proficiency is equally important. Board members must bring a unique set of skills and expertise to the table. They should be able to provide guidance, make informed decisions, and offer advice based on their experience and knowledge. It is also essential that board members have relevant connections within their respective industries, professions, or communities, as these connections can help the organization expand its reach and influence.

When searching for ideal board members, it is essential to focus on finding individuals who align with the organization's values and possess a deep understanding of its mission. As mentioned earlier, they should be able to contribute to the organization's strategic direction, help set goals, and monitor progress toward achieving them.

Additionally, the ideal board member should be able to work collaboratively with other board members and the organization's staff. They should be able to communicate effectively and foster positive relationships with all stakeholders, including members, staff, donors, volunteers, and the wider community, industry or profession.

Again, to build a board that will serve the organization well, you need to look for individuals who embody both passion and proficiency. Here are some key qualities and characteristics to look for in great board members, why they are important, and to use as a checklist for your organization:

1. **Passion and Commitment**: Board members who are passionate about the organization's mission and committed to its success will be more engaged and dedicated to their role. They will be more likely to put in the time and effort necessary to help the organization achieve its objectives.

2. **Relevant Skills and Experience**: Board members with relevant skills and experience can provide valuable guidance and expertise to

the organization. They can bring a unique perspective and help the organization make informed decisions.

3. **Financial Literacy**: Board members should have a basic understanding of financial management, budgeting, and fundraising. This knowledge can help them make informed decisions about the organization's financial health and sustainability.

4. **Effective Communication**: Board members who can communicate effectively and collaborate well with others can help foster positive relationships with stakeholders, including donors, volunteers, and staff. They can also help ensure that the organization's message is clear and consistent.

5. **Strategic Thinking**: Board members should be able to think strategically and help set long-term goals for the organization. They should also be able to monitor progress toward achieving these goals and adjust course as needed.

6. **Integrity and Ethics**: Board members should act with integrity and uphold ethical standards in all their interactions with the organization

and its stakeholders. They should avoid conflicts of interest and act in the best interests of the organization at all times.

In summary, great board members are passionate, skilled, and committed to the organization's success. They bring a unique set of skills and experiences to the table and can provide valuable guidance and expertise. By selecting board members with these qualities and characteristics, your organization can build a strong and effective board that can help it achieve its goals and make a positive impact on its members and stakeholders.

Soft Skills Training for Board Members

Board members are selected based on their expertise, experience, and commitment to the organization's mission. While these attributes are essential, it is equally vital for them to have soft skills that enable them to work effectively as a team and make informed decisions.

Many board members are experts in their respective fields, but they may lack the necessary soft skills to serve on a board effectively. Soft skills such as conflict management, facilitation, communication, and emotional intelligence are vital in boardrooms. These skills enable them to communicate effectively, collaborate, and make informed decisions that align with the organization's mission.

In today's world, nonprofits are facing a myriad of challenges, including program development, fundraising, regulatory compliance, and changing member and donor behaviors. Board members must possess the soft skills necessary to address these challenges effectively. The lack of soft skills can lead to unproductive meetings, misunderstandings, and even board member resignations. Therefore, it is crucial to prioritize soft skills training. This is no longer a negotiable factor in an organization as the lack of these skills leads to dysfunction and dysfunction destroys organizations.

Benefits of Soft Skills Training for Board Members:

- **Enhanced Communication**: Soft skills training enhances communication and enables them to express their opinions and ideas effectively. It also ensures that they understand each other's perspectives, leading to more productive and efficient meetings.

- **Improved Decision Making**: Soft skills training helps board members to make informed decisions that align with the organization's mission. It enables them to consider various options, evaluate their pros and cons, and arrive at the best decision.

- **Conflict Resolution**: Conflict is inevitable, but soft skills training equips individuals with the skills necessary to resolve conflicts effectively. It ensures that disagreements do not derail board meetings or affect the organization's progress.

- **Better Teamwork**: Soft skills training promotes teamwork. It ensures that board members collaborate effectively, support each other, and work towards a common goal.

- **Increased Engagement**: Soft skills training increases engagement and participation in the organization's activities. It ensures that everyone is committed to the organization's mission and is working towards achieving its goals.

The following are some soft skills training that might be helpful to consider and highly recommended to maintain a functional board:

- **Conflict Management**: Conflict management training enables board members to identify, manage, and resolve conflicts effectively. It equips them with the skills necessary to handle disagreements, maintain relationships, and avoid unnecessary tensions. Issues around how to manage conflicts are the number one reason for board and staff turnover.

- **Facilitation**: Facilitation training enables board members to lead meetings effectively. It equips them with the skills necessary to manage meeting dynamics, facilitate discussions, and ensure that meetings are productive and efficient.

- **Communication**: Communication training equips board members with the skills necessary to communicate effectively. It ensures that they understand each other's perspectives and work towards a common goal.

- **Emotional Intelligence**: Emotional intelligence training enables board members to manage their emotions effectively. It equips them with the skills necessary to recognize and regulate emotions, communicate effectively, and handle conflicts constructively.

To ensure the effectiveness of boards, it is highly recommended to conduct an inventory of the necessary soft skills prior to the appointment or nomination of any board member. This process should commence with a thorough assessment of potential board members to determine the specific skills required. This assessment provides valuable insights into areas where training is needed for both hard and soft skills.

Given the critical role played by board members in achieving organizational goals, possessing the right mix of expertise, experience, and soft skills is vital. Think about developing a training plan for both hard and soft skills in order to provide board members with the tools they need to succeed before they take office. By prioritizing soft skills training, organizations can ensure that their boards are well-equipped to face the various challenges that arise and increase the chances of success at the board table. Ultimately, this investment in training will yield positive results and contribute to the overall success of the nonprofit organization.

"Missing In Action" Board Members

The Story of the Empty Board Chair by a Frustrated Board Member

Once upon a time, there was a nonprofit organization that had a dedicated board of directors. One of the board members, let's call her Sarah, was highly respected in the industry and had been nominated to the board due to her expertise in member development.

At first, Sarah was an active and engaged member of the board. She regularly attended meetings, contributed her insights, and was passionate about the organization's mission. However, as time went on, Sarah's attendance became more sporadic. She missed several meetings, was frequently absent from committee meetings, and didn't participate in any of the organization's events or fundraising efforts.

Despite repeated attempts to reach out to Sarah and get her more involved, the other board members were unable to connect with her. Sarah held a seat on the board, but she was essentially missing in action. Her chair at board meetings remained empty, and she didn't respond to emails or phone calls.

The other board members became increasingly frustrated and concerned about Sarah's lack of involvement. They were worried that the organization was missing out on the benefits of her expertise and experience in member development. Additionally, they were concerned about the message it was sending to other stakeholders, such as donors and volunteers, who might question the board's commitment to the organization's mission.

Eventually, the board made the difficult decision to remove Sarah from the board. They knew that it was not an easy decision, but they felt it was necessary to ensure the organization's success. They filled the empty chair with a new member who was enthusiastic about the organization's mission and eager to contribute to its success.

When it comes to selecting board members for a nonprofit organization, it is crucial to choose individuals who are not just present in the meetings but are also committed to doing work that advances the mission of the organization. Having passionate individuals who bring a diverse set of skills is important, but it is equally important that they are willing to commit their time and effort to actively contribute to the organization. "Missing in Action", or MIA board members, is not an option. Sometimes, no matter how much training is provided and vetting is done, MIA board members are a real problem and occupy a seat that could be provided to someone that can contribute.

Board members who are not actively engaged can hinder the progress of the organization, as their absence can result in missed opportunities for growth and development. In addition, their presence may prevent someone who is committed and dedicated from serving on the board, potentially depriving the organization of a valuable asset.

It is therefore essential to emphasize the importance of active involvement during the selection process.

This can be achieved by clearly outlining the expectations and responsibilities of board members, and emphasizing the need for regular participation in meetings and organizational activities.

It is important to establish a culture of accountability and transparency within the organization, where board members are held to high standards and are expected to actively contribute towards the goals and objectives of the organization. By doing so, the organization can ensure that they are not just taking up a seat, but are actively working towards advancing the mission and goals of the organization.

The story of the empty board chair serves as a reminder of the importance of having active and engaged board members. Even one missing or inactive member can have a significant impact on the board's ability to make informed decisions and achieve its goals. It highlights the need for all board members to be committed to the organization's mission and willing to actively participate in its activities.

Ongoing Training and Support

It's clear that providing ongoing training and support to a board of directors is a critical aspect of ensuring their success. The board, after all, is the backbone of an organization, responsible for steering its mission and overseeing its operations. But for them to do so effectively, they need the proper resources and guidance.

It's imperative, then, to prioritize their professional development by offering them workshops, retreats, and regular check-ins with staff. These opportunities not only allow the board to deepen their understanding of the organization and its goals, but also provide them with the tools they need to make informed decisions.

In a rapidly changing world, it's crucial that the board stays abreast of developments in their field, as well as best practices in governance and leadership. Regular training can also provide an opportunity for the board to build relationships and foster a sense of community, which can only strengthen their resolve and commitment to the organization's mission.

A board training and development workshop, which should occur annually, should include a range of topics and activities aimed at equipping board members with the knowledge, skills, and understanding they need to fulfill their responsibilities effectively. This is in addition to the soft skills training described earlier.

Here are a few key components that should be included:

- **Overview of the organization's mission, vision, values, and goals:** This provides a foundation for understanding why the organization exists, where it wants to go, and what it hopes to achieve.
- **Understanding of the board's role and responsibilities:** This includes a clear explanation of the duties of individual board members and the responsibilities of the board as a whole.
- **Effective board and staff relationships:** This can include discussions on building trust, setting expectations, and resolving conflicts.

Having a healthy relationship between the board and staff can lead to better decision-making, improved organizational performance, and a more effective implementation of the mission statement.

- **Overview of governance practices:** This covers best practices for effective governance, including financial management, risk management, and board-staff relations.

- **Understanding of the legal and regulatory environment:** This includes information on relevant laws and regulations that impact the organization, such as tax laws, charity regulations, and labor laws.

- **Building skills for effective decision-making:** This can include workshops on strategic planning, risk management, and conflict resolution.

- **Risk management:** Board members can learn about different types of risks, how to assess and mitigate them, and how to develop a risk management strategy that aligns with the organization's mission and goals.

- **Opportunities for peer learning and networking:** This provides board members with the opportunity to share their experiences and perspectives, learn from others, and build relationships with their fellow board members.

- **Regular check-ins and feedback:** This includes opportunities for board members to provide feedback on their training and development needs, as well as regular check-ins to monitor their progress and ensure they are supported in their role.

In short, providing ongoing training and support to the board is a vital investment in the long-term success of the organization. By giving them the tools they need to succeed, they can make a lasting impact and ensure the organization's mission is fulfilled.

Why a Culture of Collaboration Is Important

A culture of collaboration among the board and staff is essential as it fosters trust, teamwork, and a shared sense of purpose. It helps to create an environment where everyone feels heard, valued, and engaged, leading to better decision-making and problem solving, and can also result in a more effective and efficient use of resources, as well as improved relationships with stakeholders.

It is essential to cultivate a culture of unity and collaboration within the organization, promoting a "one team" mentality that prioritizes the achievement of the mission over individual interests.

Ultimately, a culture of collaboration is a critical aspect of effective governance which helps to ensure the success and sustainability of the organization by enabling the board and staff to work together towards a common goal.

The following steps can help foster a collaborative environment:

- **Define and communicate the desired culture:** The board should clearly communicate its vision for collaboration, including the values and behaviors that are expected of all members. This can help set the tone for open communication and teamwork.
- **Encourage active participation:** All board members should feel comfortable sharing their

opinions, asking questions, and engaging in discussions. Encouraging active participation helps to build trust and creates a sense of shared ownership among the board.

- **Foster open communication:** Encouraging open and honest communication helps to build trust and strengthens relationships between board members. The board should establish regular check-ins, debriefs, and evaluations to ensure that all members have an opportunity to share their thoughts and feedback.

- **Foster a culture of continuous learning:** A culture of continuous learning helps board members to stay current with new developments in their field and to expand their knowledge and skills. The board should regularly provide training and development opportunities, such as workshops and conferences, to help members stay engaged and up to date.

- **Establish clear roles and responsibilities:** Establishing clear roles and responsibilities helps to minimize confusion and ensures that all members are working towards the same goals. The board should establish a clear decision-making process and delegate responsibilities appropriately.

By following these steps, a board can build a culture of collaboration that supports effective decision-making, maximizes the impact of the organization, and fosters a positive working environment for all members.

Ensuring Effective Governance

Good governance is the foundation of any organization, and it's what sets successful organizations apart from those that struggle to stay afloat. Effective governance is not only crucial for the long-term health of the organization, but it also plays a vital role in building trust with stakeholders, including members, volunteers, staff, and the wider community.

At its core, good governance is about having strong policies in place to guide decision-making and ensure that the organization is operating in a responsible and ethical manner. This includes everything from financial management and risk management to human resources and legal compliance. Having clear policies and procedures in place provides a roadmap for the board and staff to follow, and it helps to mitigate the risk of costly mistakes or ethical violations.

In addition to having strong policies in place, regular self-assessment is also crucial to ensuring effective governance. Self-assessment provides an opportunity for the board to reflect on its performance, identify areas for improvement, and make changes as needed to ensure that the organization is operating at its best. This can be done through regular board evaluations, as well as regular assessments of the policies and procedures themselves.

Also, a commitment to ethical behavior is essential for good governance. The board is responsible for setting the tone for the organization and ensuring that all decisions are made with integrity and in the best interest of the organization. This includes adhering to high ethical standards, as well as being transparent and accountable in all decision-making processes.

There are several key policies that organizations can put in place to ensure effective governance, responsible decision-making, and ethical behavior. These include:

- **Code of Ethics:** A clear code of ethics outlines the values and principles that guide the organization and provides a framework for ethical decision-making.

- **Conflict of Interest Policy:** A conflict of interest policy helps prevent conflicts between personal and organizational interests, ensuring that decisions are made in the best interests of the organization.

- **Risk Management Policy:** A risk management policy identifies potential risks and outlines procedures for mitigating those risks, protecting the organization from harm.

- **Financial Management Policies:** Policies on financial management, such as budgeting and auditing, help ensure that resources are being used effectively and efficiently.

- **Transparency and Accountability Policy:** A commitment to transparency and accountability helps build trust with stakeholders, ensuring that the organization is operating in an open and responsible manner.

- **Board and Staff Evaluation Policy:** Regular evaluations of the board and staff help ensure that the organization is making progress towards its goals and that individuals are fulfilling their responsibilities effectively.

- **Whistleblower Policy:** A whistleblower policy provides a mechanism for individuals to report unethical behavior or misconduct, protecting the organization from harm.

Having these policies in place provides a framework for decision-making and helps ensure that the organization is operating in a responsible and ethical manner. Regular reviews of these policies and procedures can help ensure they remain relevant and effective over time. In fact, the Internal Revenue Service (IRS) also recommends that nonprofit boards have these policies in place and failing to implement them could potentially result in legal and financial consequences for the board and the organization.

"Gavel to Gavel" Authority

As a governing body, the board of directors holds a significant amount of power when they are together at an official meeting. The key phrase is "when they are together". This power is known as "gavel to gavel authority" and it refers to the ability of the board to transact official business during the time that the gavel is dropped to open the meeting until the gavel is dropped to close the meeting.

During this time, the board has the power to make decisions, approve policies and budgets, and set the direction of the organization as a body. It's important to note that no individual board member has more power than another during this time unless the board has vested that power in a particular board member.

However, outside of the official meeting, each board member has no individual power to change the direction of the board. Board members have a fiduciary duty to act in the best interest of the organization, and any decisions must be made collectively during an official meeting.

When the board leaves a meeting, they must respect and support the decisions made during that meeting, even if they did not necessarily agree with them. Failure to do so can cause significant harm to the organization and undermine the authority of the board as a collective.

Unfortunately, there have been instances where individual board members have not respected the decisions made during a meeting and have taken it upon themselves to speak with members of the organization outside of the meeting and say how horrible the board is and how many bad decisions they have made. This can cause significant harm to the organization and create confusion and discord. This is unacceptable and cause for removal.

For example, consider a scenario where the board of a nonprofit organization has decided to allocate funds towards a particular program. However, a board member who did not agree with the decision starts speaking with members of the organization, expressing their dissent and causing others to question the decision. This can lead to a lack of confidence in the organization's leadership and a breakdown in the decision-making process.

It's important for board members to understand their role as part of the board and to respect the power of the board as a collective and governing body. By doing so, they can ensure that the organization operates effectively and in the best interest of its stakeholders.

Danger of Assuming Unilateral Power as Board President

While the board of directors operates with "gavel to gavel authority," it's important to understand that this power is held collectively by the board as a governing body and not by any individual member, including the board president or chair. Unfortunately, there have been instances where board presidents or chairs have assumed that they have more power than they actually do, making decisions unilaterally and without board approval.

This type of behavior is not only inappropriate, but it can also be damaging to the organization. The board president or chair is not a dictator, but rather a facilitator of the decision-making process. They must work collaboratively with the rest of the board to ensure that decisions are made collectively and in the best interest of the organization.

For example, consider a scenario where a new board president comes on board and announces that they have their own goals for the organization, without consulting the rest of the board or considering the strategic plan that had already been approved by the governing body. This type of behavior not only undermines the authority of the board, but it also creates confusion and mistrust among board members and stakeholders.

The board president or chair must understand that their role is to guide the board in fulfilling its responsibilities, not to make decisions unilaterally. Any decisions made by the board president or chair must be made in consultation with the rest of the board and must be consistent with the organization's bylaws, mission, and strategic plan.

It's also important to note that the board president or chair serves at the pleasure of the board and can be removed from their position if they fail to fulfill their duties. This underscores the importance of understanding the collective power of the board and the need for collaboration and consensus-building.

In conclusion, the board president or chair plays a critical role in the decision-making process, but they must do so in collaboration with the rest of the board. Assuming unilateral power can be damaging to the organization and undermines the collective authority of the board.

How To Fire a Board Member

Firing a nonprofit board member is a difficult decision that should not be taken lightly. However, there are times when it may be necessary to ensure the success of the organization.

Reasons for firing a board member may include a lack of attendance, failure to fulfill their duties, conflicts of interest, or behavior that is harmful to the organization's reputation. Whatever the reason, the decision to terminate a board member's tenure must be based on clear and documented evidence.

Taking the necessary steps to terminate a board member's tenure can be a challenging and uncomfortable process. However, it is a fiduciary responsibility of the board to ensure that the organization's best interests are being served.

Here are the steps to follow when considering firing a nonprofit board member:

1. **Review the organization's bylaws**: The bylaws should outline the procedures for removing a board member. Follow these procedures carefully to ensure that the process is fair and legally sound.
2. **Document the reasons for termination**: Gather evidence that supports the decision to terminate the board member. This documentation should be objective and verifiable, such as attendance records or meeting minutes.
3. **Meet with the board member**: Arrange a meeting with the board member to discuss the

situation. Explain the reasons for the termination and give the board member an opportunity to respond.

4. **Vote on the decision**: After considering the board member's response, the board should vote on the decision to terminate their tenure. The vote should be recorded in the meeting minutes.

5. **Inform the board member**: Inform the board member of the decision in writing. Be professional and respectful in the communication, and provide a clear explanation for the decision.

6. **Take steps to fill the vacancy**: Once the board member has been removed, take steps to fill the vacancy. This may include appointing a new board member or conducting a search for a replacement.

One strategy may be to include some pre-emptive steps in bylaws. In some cases, it may be beneficial for an organization to include provisions in their bylaws that allow for automatic removal of board members in certain circumstances. For example, if a board member has a certain number of unexcused absences from board meetings, they could be automatically removed from the board. This can help to ensure that board members are fulfilling their duties and attending meetings regularly.

It's important to note that any provisions included in the bylaws for automatic removal must be in compliance with the organization's state laws and regulations. It's recommended to consult with legal counsel to ensure that any automatic removal provisions are legally sound.

If automatic removal provisions are included in the bylaws, it's still important to follow the appropriate procedures listed earlier for removing a board member. This includes documenting the absences or other reasons for removal and notifying the board member of the decision in writing.

The decision to include automatic removal provisions in the bylaws is up to the organization's board of directors. However, it can be a useful tool for ensuring that board members are fulfilling their duties and maintaining the integrity of the organization.

Firing a nonprofit board member is a difficult decision that should only be made after careful consideration and with clear documentation to support the decision. While it may be uncomfortable (don't forget the soft skills!), it is a fiduciary responsibility of the board to ensure that the organization's best interests are being served. By following these steps, the board can ensure that the process is fair, legally sound, and respectful to all parties involved. It should not be ignored because it is hard to do but it should be done because it is the legal, fiduciary responsibility of a board to do so.

Chapter Four: Developing a Strategic Plan

A comprehensive strategic plan is essential for navigating the path towards realizing an organization's mission and effecting positive change in the community or industry it serves. It enables organizations to zero in on the most critical priorities and focus their efforts and resources accordingly. A well-conceived strategic plan not only outlines the direction of the organization but also serves as a roadmap to guide its progress and ensure successful outcomes.

Having a clear vision and mission that is communicated to everyone involved in the organization—from staff and volunteers to stakeholders, supporters, and members—is a critical component of a successful strategic plan. This allows everyone to work together towards a common goal and ensures that everyone is aligned and motivated.

Moreover, a strong strategic plan helps to optimize resources, prioritize initiatives, and measure progress over time. This helps to ensure that the organization is effectively allocating its resources to the areas that will have the greatest impact.

In addition, a well-crafted strategic plan can help build trust with stakeholders, members, and supporters who want to know that their investments of time, money, and resources are being used effectively. It gives stakeholders and supporters a sense of ownership and pride in the organization and its mission.

A strong strategic plan is a critical tool for any nonprofit looking to create real and lasting change. It helps organizations to focus on what truly matters, aligns everyone towards a common goal, and sets the stage for long-term success.

Strong Elements of a Strategic Plan

A nonprofit's success depends on many factors, but one of the most important is having a well-structured and effective strategic plan. As we have said many times, it serves as a roadmap, guiding the organization towards its goals and helping it navigate the challenges along the way. By establishing clear objectives and actionable steps, a strong strategic plan ensures that resources are used wisely and that progress is made towards the organization's mission.

In this chapter, we will delve into the following key components of a successful strategic plan and discuss the steps that need to be taken to ensure its effectiveness:

- Defining the organization's mission, vision, and values.
- Identifying and prioritizing goals and objectives.
- Assessing strengths, weaknesses, opportunities, and threats (SWOT analysis).
- Developing and implementing action plans.
- Regular monitoring and evaluation.
- Continuous improvement and adaptation.

Defining the Organization's Mission, Vision, and Values

It's crucial for an organization to define its mission, vision, and values to set a clear direction and create a lasting impact. These three elements are interdependent and play a vital role in shaping the organization's purpose, culture, and strategy. Here's how to define each of these elements:

- **Mission:** The mission of an organization should be a clear statement that explains why the organization exists and what it intends to achieve. It should be concise and inspiring, providing a shared purpose for everyone within the organization.

- **Vision:** The vision should articulate the organization's aspirations for the future. It should be ambitious and provide a picture of what success looks like in the long-term. A vision should be aspirational, inspiring, and provide direction for the organization.

- **Values:** The values of an organization should be a set of guiding principles that define how the organization conducts itself and interacts with others. These values should be reflected in the organization's culture, decision-making processes, and day-to-day operations.

Defining these elements requires careful consideration and buy-in from everyone inside and outside of the organization. Once defined, they should be communicated effectively to ensure everyone understands the organization's direction and purpose. This clarity will help to build a culture of alignment, accountability, and momentum towards the achievement of the organization's goals.

Identifying and Prioritizing Goals and Strategies

It's critical to understand that setting goals and strategies is at the core of any successful strategic plan. It is the roadmap that guides decision-making and ensures that everyone is working towards a common purpose.

The foundation of effective goal setting and strategy formulation for a nonprofit organization lies in a thorough understanding of its distinct circumstances and priorities aligned with its mission. This allows for a focused approach towards realizing the organization's aspirations and making a meaningful impact.

To begin the strategic planning process, it is crucial to conduct a comprehensive analysis of the organization's internal and external factors using a SWOT analysis.

The SWOT analysis (a widely used strategy in organizational planning) was first developed by Albert Humphrey, a consultant and researcher at the Stanford Research Institute, in the mid-20th century.

The SWOT analysis is a tool that helps organizations evaluate their internal and external factors, such as strengths, weaknesses, opportunities, and threats, in order to make informed decisions about their future. This method has become a staple in business and organizational planning due to its simplicity and effectiveness in assessing organizational performance and potential. A SWOT analysis will provide a clear understanding of the context in which the organization operates and the most pressing challenges and opportunities it faces.

Next, it is essential to engage in a collaborative effort to set and prioritize goals that align with the organization's mission and values and support its strategies. A useful framework to consider is the SMART goal setting method.

The SMART goals concept is widely credited to George Doran, a management consultant who first introduced the concept in a 1981 article in the *Management Review*. The SMART acronym stands for Specific, Measurable, Achievable, Relevant, and Time-bound, and the concept outlines a framework for setting goals that are clear, actionable, and achievable.

Since its introduction, the SMART goals concept has become a widely-adopted tool for goal setting in businesses, organizations, and personal development contexts, and is considered a key component of effective goal setting and performance management. It is also crucial to set performance measures for each strategy, as this will allow for fine-tuning of the goals and strategies as they relate to each other.

It is important to involve key stakeholders, such as staff, board members, volunteers, and other critical parties, in this process to ensure that goals and strategies reflect the perspectives of those who will be impacted by them, and to foster support and buy-in.

Ultimately, the key to successfully identifying and prioritizing goals and objectives is to engage in a structured and inclusive process that takes into account the organization's unique circumstances and focuses on what is most critical to achieving its mission. With a clear understanding of its goals and strategies, the organization can make informed decisions and take effective action to advance its mission and achieve its objectives.

Consider Replacing SMART Goals with SMART Strategies

As detailed earlier, in many organizations, the concept of setting SMART goals has become an integral part of the planning process. However, while SMART goals are useful for establishing specific, measurable, achievable, relevant, and time-bound objectives, they may not be sufficient for achieving the desired outcomes. Instead, organizations should consider diving deeper into SMART strategies and how they can be even more important than SMART goals.

Unlike goals, which are often broad and high-level, strategies provide a more specific and actionable plan for achieving a desired outcome. By setting SMART strategies, organizations can ensure that their resources, activities, and tactics are aligned with their goals and are being used in the most effective and efficient way possible.

Furthermore, SMART strategies provide a framework for accountability, helping to measure progress and ensure that the organization is on track to achieve its goals. Each strategy can be held accountable and measured against its progress, allowing the organization to identify areas of success and areas that need improvement. This information can then be used to make informed decisions, adjust course as needed, and ultimately achieve the desired outcomes.

In summary, while SMART goals have their place in the planning process, organizations should consider replacing the concept of setting SMART goals with setting SMART strategies. By doing so, they can ensure that their actions are aligned with their goals, and they have a specific and actionable plan for achieving the desired outcomes.

Importance of an Effective SWOT Analysis

Previously, we highlighted the significance of the SWOT analysis and its concept. It is imperative to comprehend the significance of conducting this analysis, as it serves as a comprehensive evaluation of an organization's internal and external factors.

By examining the strengths, weaknesses, opportunities, and threats, organizations gain a clear understanding of their current reality and are better equipped to identify their most pressing challenges and opportunities. This step in the strategic planning process is crucial as it helps organizations to make informed decisions and move forward with confidence towards their mission and goals.

The SWOT analysis provides a roadmap to guide the organization's decision-making process, enabling it to capitalize on its strengths, address its weaknesses, take advantage of opportunities, and mitigate the threats it faces.

By thoroughly examining these four key areas, an organization can create a strategic plan that is grounded in reality, enabling it to effectively allocate its resources and set achievable goals. A SWOT analysis is therefore an essential tool that helps organizations to move from a state of uncertainty to a state of clarity, providing a clear direction for the future.

Crafting a Strategic Action Plan That Works

In the world of strategy, a well-crafted action plan is the cornerstone of successful implementation. It lays out a clear roadmap for how an organization will turn its goals and objectives into tangible, measurable results. Without an action plan, even the most brilliant strategic plan is nothing more than a collection of good intentions.

A strategic plan is only as valuable as its ability to be put into action. An action plan is crucial because it takes the broad, abstract goals and objectives of the organization and breaks them down into concrete, achievable steps. Without an action plan, a strategic plan can simply remain a dream, gathering dust on a shelf.

So, why is an action plan important in a strategic plan? An action plan provides the necessary framework for the organization to turn its aspirations into reality. It acts as a roadmap, helping the organization to focus its resources, prioritize its efforts, and measure its progress. An action plan also provides accountability and helps to keep the organization on track, making sure that everyone involved is focused on achieving the same goals.

The steps in creating an action plan are as follows:

1. Start by reviewing the organization's mission, vision, values, goals, and strategies.
2. Determine the key activities, tasks, and responsibilities necessary to achieve each goal and objective.

3. Prioritize each item to ensure the highest mission impact, knowing that the organization has limited resources.
4. Assign an accountable person or team responsible for each activity, task, or responsibility.
5. Identify a timeline for completion and establish milestones or markers to measure progress.
6. Define any resources required, such as funding, personnel, or technology.
7. Identify any potential obstacles and plan for how to overcome them.
8. Implement a systematic approach for monitoring and reporting progress, such as frequent updates or a yearly assessment. An accessible dashboard presented at each board meeting would provide optimal visibility and accountability.

By following these steps, an organization can ensure that its action plan is comprehensive, realistic, and achievable. With a solid action plan in place, an organization can be confident that its strategic plan will be more than just a collection of aspirations—it will become a blueprint for success.

Regular Monitoring and Evaluation

It is crucial for organizations to regularly monitor and evaluate their strategic plan to ensure its effectiveness and success. This is not simply a matter of checking boxes or ticking off items on a list, but rather a critical step in the ongoing journey of growth and improvement.

Dashboards are a powerful tool for monitoring progress against strategic goals and objectives. They provide a visual representation of key metrics and performance indicators, and should be presented at every board meeting to keep the board informed about progress towards achieving organizational goals.

To create an effective dashboard, organizations must first identify the most important metrics and KPIs that align with their strategic plan. This requires a deep understanding of the organization's mission, vision, and values, as well as a clear sense of the key outcomes and impacts that the strategic plan is seeking to achieve.

Once the metrics have been identified, the next step is to design a dashboard that clearly and accurately communicates this information in a way that is easy to understand and actionable. This might involve using charts, graphs, and other visual aids to present the data in a compelling and meaningful way.

Regular monitoring and evaluation is essential for any strategic plan, as it provides organizations with a way to track progress, identify areas for improvement, and make course corrections as needed. By using dashboards to provide a clear and concise picture of performance, organizations can more effectively understand their progress and make informed decisions about how to improve.

Ultimately, the goal of regular monitoring and evaluation is to ensure that the strategic plan is aligned with the organization's mission, vision, and values, and that it is driving meaningful results and outcomes. By taking the time to review and refine the plan on an ongoing basis, organizations can maintain their focus, stay on track, and achieve their most ambitious goals and objectives.

Continuous Improvement and Adaptation

In the world of nonprofit organizations, change is the only constant. That's why it's essential to have a strategic plan that not only outlines goals and strategies, but also accommodates for that change. This is where the concept of continuous improvement and adaptation comes in.

A well-crafted strategic plan is a vital tool for navigating the future of any organization. However, the path to success is often dotted with unexpected obstacles and detours that can impact progress. To ensure continued alignment with the organization's mission and goals, it is crucial to adopt a culture of continuous improvement and adaptation.

This requires regularly reviewing and adjusting the plan to reflect changes in the internal and external environment. Proactivity in seeking opportunities to improve is key in maintaining the relevancy and effectiveness of the strategic plan.

To facilitate this process, the use of performance metrics and dashboards can provide a visual representation of progress and allow for quick and informed decision-making. These metrics should be regularly reviewed at board meetings to ensure the plan remains on track.

A strong strategic plan is not a one-time effort, but a living document that evolves with the growth and development of the organization. By embracing continuous review, adjustment, and monitoring, the plan remains relevant and effective, leading the organization towards its mission and goals.

What to Do If the Plan Goes "Off the Rails"

It is important to understand that even the best-laid plans can sometimes go off-track. When this happens, it's important to quickly assess the situation and take the necessary steps to get things back on track:

1. **Identify the root cause:** Determine why the plan is off track—whether it's due to changes in the environment, internal challenges, or something else.

2. **Evaluate the impact:** Assess the impact of the situation on the organization's mission, goals, and strategies.

3. **Re-prioritize:** Determine which elements of the plan need to be re-prioritized to get back on track and make any necessary adjustments.

4. **Communicate:** Ensure that all stakeholders are aware of the situation and the steps being taken to address it.

5. **Monitor progress:** Regularly monitor progress and assess the effectiveness of the steps taken to get the plan back on track.

It is important to approach a situation where a strategic plan goes off track with a sense of urgency, but also with a clear head. By taking the time to evaluate the situation and determine the best course of action, the organization can get back on track and continue working towards its mission and goals.

Committees and Task Forces for Plan Execution

To maximize the impact of a strategic plan, it is essential to leverage the power of committees and task forces. These groups serve as the driving force behind the execution of the plan and play a crucial role in ensuring the realization of the organization's vision. It is important to utilize their expertise and energy to effectively bring the strategic plan to life.

Committees and task forces can be highly effective because they bring together individuals with specific skills and expertise to tackle specific objectives. By dividing the work into smaller, manageable pieces, your organization can make more significant progress towards its overall goals.

But it's important to remember that committees and task forces are only effective if they are structured and managed correctly. Here are a few key principles to keep in mind when using these tools to execute your strategic plan:

- **Clearly define roles and responsibilities:** Each committee or task force should have a clear and specific purpose, and each member should know their role and what they are responsible for.
- **Provide adequate support:** Committees and task forces need resources, both human and

financial, to be successful. Make sure your committees have the support they need to carry out their objectives.

- **Establish clear goals and objectives:** Each committee or task force should have specific and measurable goals and strategies that are one hundred percent aligned with the overall strategic plan.

- **Foster collaboration and communication:** Members of committees and task forces should work together and communicate effectively to ensure everyone is working towards the same goal.

- **Provide regular feedback and assessment:** Regular feedback and assessment are critical to ensure committees and task forces are making progress and staying on track. Regular reports and updates should be provided to the board and professional staff team.

These core principles can be utilized to effectively implement a strategic plan through the use of committees and task forces. This approach facilitates the division of work into manageable portions, while also leveraging the specialized knowledge and capabilities of individual team members, leading to successful realization of the organization's vision and mission.

Managing Rogue Committees and Task Forces

First, always keep in mind that it is the fiduciary role of the board to set the strategic direction of the organization through a strategic plan. If a committee or task force goes "rogue" and moves in an entirely different direction from the board-approved strategic plan, it is important to quickly identify the issue and take action.

The first step is to assess the situation and determine the root cause of the problem. This could be due to a lack of clear direction, misaligned priorities, or ineffective communication and collaboration.

Once the cause has been identified, it's time to take action. This may involve adjusting the committee's mandate, replacing key members, or re-focusing the group's efforts on a more achievable goal.

It's also important to ensure that clear lines of communication are established, and that all members are aligned with the mission and goals of the task force. It is important to acknowledge that in business, decisions should be based on facts and objectives, rather than emotions or personal considerations. Ignoring an issue may cause more harm in the long run and it is important to address it in a professional and straightforward manner to ensure the success of the organization.

Another critical aspect of getting a committee or task force back on track is to maintain focus on the organization's mission, vision, and values. As we noted earlier, this means that the work of the committee should be directly tied to the goals of the organization, and that the decisions made are in line with its overall strategy and tactics. The committee or task force must align fully with the organization's strategic plan and not develop its own independent strategies outside of the plan. This ensures that all efforts and initiatives are in line with the overarching objectives and vision of the organization.

Ultimately, the key to ensuring that a committee or task force remains focused and productive is to have a clear plan in place with board-dedicated resources and to regularly monitor and evaluate progress. This may involve setting up a system for tracking milestones and progress, as well as regularly scheduled meetings to assess progress and make adjustments as necessary. This is where a dashboard is so effective.

With this in mind, organizations can be confident that their committees and task forces are working effectively to achieve their goals.

Chapter Five: Sustainable Revenue and Finances

As someone who works with many organizations in the nonprofit sector, I've seen that obtaining sustainable revenue and finances for growth is a critical challenge for all nonprofits, regardless of size or focus.

This challenge exists as it's a paradox of the nonprofit world. On one hand, nonprofits exist to serve a cause that is greater than themselves—to make a positive impact on their communities, the professions, and industries they serve, while creating a better world. Yet, to do this effectively, they need to have stable, reliable, and growing sources of funding. Without adequate resources, their impact is limited, and their ability to deliver on their mission is at risk.

The reasons for this challenge are many.

First, nonprofits often operate in highly competitive environments, where they are competing for the same dollars with other organizations or worthy causes.

Second, they must balance their desire to do good with the need to be financially responsible, to build a strong brand, and to earn the trust of their members and stakeholders.

But, perhaps the greatest challenge is that nonprofits are often under-resourced when it comes to revenue development and marketing expertise. They may not have the staff, the skills, or the budget to develop a robust revenue growth strategy, or to implement it effectively. This creates a vicious cycle, where they cannot grow their revenues because they lack the capacity, and they cannot build that capacity because they cannot grow their revenues.

Ultimately, the key to overcoming these challenges is to take a strategic and intentional approach to building sustainable revenue and finances for growth. This requires a deep understanding of the organization's mission, vision, and values, as well as a clear sense of the resources, skills, and opportunities that are available. It also requires a willingness to experiment, learn, and adapt, as well as a relentless focus on results.

This chapter will delve into some effective strategies and tactics proven to be successful.

Diversify Revenue Streams

Diversifying revenue streams is a key strategy for ensuring sustainable revenue and growth for nonprofits, including membership organizations. Here are some steps that organizations can follow to diversify their revenue streams:

- **Assess the current revenue mix:** Review the current sources of revenue and identify areas for improvement. This will help determine which new revenue streams to explore.
- **Identify potential revenue streams:** Consider a mix of grants, sponsorships, memberships, events, and products or services as potential sources of revenue. Evaluate which ones align with the organization's mission and resources, and which have the potential to generate significant revenue.
- **Develop a plan for each revenue stream:** For each potential revenue stream, develop a plan

that outlines the steps required to launch and scale the stream. Consider factors such as resources required, target audience, marketing and outreach strategies, and expected results.

- **Test and refine:** Launch small-scale pilots for each new revenue stream and measure the results. Based on the results, refine the plans and scale up the successful streams.

- **Regularly review and adjust:** Regularly review the revenue mix and make adjustments as needed. This will help ensure that the organization remains on track and that the revenue streams remain relevant and effective.

- **Foster partnerships and collaborations:** Collaborate with other organizations, businesses, and individuals to jointly develop and promote new revenue streams.

Impact and Importance of Scaling

Scaling is the process of increasing the reach and impact of an organization's programs, benefits, and services to a larger audience without sacrificing quality. It is an important strategy for nonprofit organizations that seek to maximize their impact in addressing professional, business, social, environmental, or economic challenges.

Scaling involves a deliberate and systematic approach to expanding an organization's reach and impact while maintaining the effectiveness of its programs. This can be achieved through a variety of strategies, including leveraging technology, building strategic partnerships, replicating successful programs in new locations, and increasing funding and resources.

Scaling can help nonprofit organizations achieve greater efficiency, increase their social impact, and ultimately achieve their mission. By scaling their programs, benefits, and services, organizations can serve more people, create more meaningful change, and make a bigger impact in the communities they serve.

To successfully scale, nonprofit organizations must have a clear understanding of their goals, objectives, and target audience, as well as the resources and capacity needed to implement their scaling strategy. They must also be willing to adapt and iterate their programs and services as they expand to new audiences, ensuring that they remain effective and responsive to the needs of their beneficiaries.

One example of a nonprofit that scaled its program is Teach For America (TFA), an organization that recruits and trains college graduates to teach in under-resourced schools across the United States.

TFA began as a small program in 1990 with just over 100 teachers in six cities. Over time, the organization grew in popularity and expanded its reach, recruiting more and more teachers each year. By 2018, TFA had placed over 60,000 teachers in classrooms across the country, and had become one of the largest educational nonprofits in the world.

To scale its program, TFA focused on building strong partnerships with schools and school districts, as well as investing in technology and training to support its teachers. The organization also worked to expand its funding sources and raise awareness of its mission, which helped to attract more recruits and supporters.

Overall, TFA's success in scaling its program highlights the importance of building strategic partnerships, investing in technology and training, and building a strong brand to attract support and funding. Scaling is a key strategy for nonprofit organizations seeking to maximize their impact and create meaningful change in the world.

Building a Strong Relationship with Donors

Though crucial to the success of any organization, organizations that rely mostly on grants and individual contributions need to build strong relationships with donors. Donors are the lifeblood of foundations, providing much-needed financial support, and it's essential that organizations foster meaningful connections with them.

Here are some strategies that have been observed to be effective:

- **Personalizing the approach**: Donors value feeling appreciated, and a personalized approach can establish a strong relationship. It is important to take the time to understand each donor's interests and motivations.

- **Keeping donors informed**: Consistent communication is crucial in maintaining donor engagement. Providing updates on the organization's progress, accomplishments, and future plans can help to keep donors engaged.

- **Recognizing and thanking donors**: Display gratitude for donations, regardless of the amount. A simple thank-you note or a personalized message can help build a strong relationship.

- **Providing opportunities for engagement**: Offer opportunities for donors to engage with the organization through events, volunteer opportunities, or advocacy campaigns.

- **Being transparent**: Building trust involves being transparent about the organization's finances, governance, and decision-making processes.

- **Being responsive**: Responding promptly to donor questions or concerns demonstrates a commitment to building a strong partnership.

- **Continuously evaluating and improving**: Regularly assessing and evaluating the donor relationship, while seeking feedback and making necessary adjustments, can lead to improved outcomes.

Building strong relationships with donors takes effort and commitment, but it is well worth the investment. By fostering meaningful connections, nonprofits can build a loyal donor base, which is essential to their long-term success.

Effective Membership Development Strategies

To implement effective membership development strategies, a nonprofit must first understand its target audience and the motivations behind why people choose to become members. This requires a deep understanding of the needs and values of a nonprofit's members, and a commitment to meeting those needs in meaningful ways.

One of the keys to success is clear and effective communication. Regular, personalized communication with members is essential to building trust and maintaining engagement. Organizations should also be proactive in seeking feedback and using it to improve the member experience.

Another important factor is providing unparalleled value. Organizations must work to create just-in-time programs and services that meet the specific needs and provide tangible benefits that justify its cost. Members shouldn't have to wait until the next event to derive value. In addition, organizations can create opportunities for members to connect and engage with each other, further strengthening the sense of community and connection to the organization.

Organizations must also be flexible and responsive to changing needs and circumstances. This may mean regularly reviewing and updating benefits and services to ensure they are relevant and effective. It may also involve adapting marketing and recruitment strategies to reach new or different audiences.

On the flip side, I've seen organizations lose members. Some common root causes include:

- **Lack of engagement:** Members may lose interest in the organization if they don't feel connected to its mission, or if they don't receive regular communications or opportunities to get involved.

- **Poor value proposition:** If the benefits don't align with what members are looking for, they may decide to let their membership lapse.

- **Poor customer service:** If they have questions or concerns that go unanswered or unaddressed, they may decide to disengage from the organization.

- **Lack of relevance:** If the organization's offerings, programs, or initiatives are not relevant to their interests or needs, they may not see the value in staying engaged.

- **Competition:** If there are other organizations that offer similar benefits and opportunities in a better or more efficient and effective way than your organization, members may opt to direct their attention and resources elsewhere.

- **Cost:** If the membership fee is too high, or if members feel that the value they receive is not worth the investment, they may choose not to renew.

By understanding these root causes and taking steps to address them, nonprofits can work to minimize attrition and build lasting relationships with their members. Ultimately, successful membership development requires a holistic, data-driven approach that is constantly evolving and adapting to changing needs.

Utilizing Data-Driven Decision-Making

As an experienced observer of nonprofit challenges, it is strongly believed that the implementation of data-driven decision-making can significantly contribute to the diversification of revenue streams. By relying on data and facts, organizations can make informed decisions, rather than relying on guesswork or assumptions.

Data-driven decision making is a process of making these informed and effective decisions based on the analysis and interpretation of data and facts. It involves collecting, processing, and analyzing data to extract meaningful insights and information that can be used to guide decision-making processes. By relying on data-driven insights, organizations can avoid biases and guesswork, and instead make informed decisions that lead to more efficient and effective outcomes. The use of data-driven decision making is increasingly recognized as a powerful tool for organizations seeking to achieve their goals and objectives in a rapidly changing and complex world.

Here are some strategies that can help organizations make informed decisions based on data:

- **Track performance:** Regularly collect and analyze data on key performance indicators, such as donor and member retention, conversion rates, and revenue generated from different sources. This information can provide valuable insights into what's working well and where there may be opportunities for improvement.

- **Conduct market research:** Understanding the organization's target audience, competition, and market trends can inform revenue diversification strategies. Conduct surveys, focus groups, or other types of market research to gather data and inform decisions.

- **Analyze past successes and failures:** Take a closer look at the organization's past efforts, including what worked well and what didn't.

Use this information to inform future strategies and avoid repeating past mistakes.

- **Collect feedback from stakeholders:** Regularly seek input from stakeholders, including donors, members, and staff, to gather valuable insights into what they think is working well and what could be improved.

- **Invest in technology:** Utilizing technology to collect and analyze data can save time and resources and increase the accuracy of your data. Consider investing in tools and platforms that can automate data collection, analysis, and reporting.

One example of an organization that used data-driven decision making to tackle a significant challenge is a professional association that represents over 4 million registered healthcare professionals. The association faced a declining membership rate and needed to address the issue proactively.

To tackle the challenge, the association conducted a comprehensive analysis of its membership data, including demographics, engagement levels, and feedback from member surveys. The data analysis revealed that many members were not engaged with the association and did not feel their needs were being met.

Using these insights, the association developed a targeted member engagement program, providing personalized experiences and resources based on individual needs and interests. The association also invested significantly in its technology infrastructure to support more efficient and effective communication and engagement with members. As a result of implementing a data-driven approach to member engagement and retention, the organization was able to address the issue of declining membership rates effectively. The targeted member engagement program, based on personalized experiences and resources, helped increase member engagement and retention.

Additionally, the investment in technology infrastructure supported more efficient and effective communication and engagement with members.

Key Takeaways:

- Data-driven decision-making can help organizations identify challenges and opportunities more effectively.
- Comprehensive data analysis can provide insights that may not be immediately apparent and help an organization prioritize its efforts.
- Personalized experiences and resources can increase member engagement and retention.
- Investing in technology infrastructure can support more efficient and effective communication and engagement with members.

The organization's successful use of data-driven decision making serves as an excellent example of how organizations can leverage data insights to improve their operations and achieve their goals.

Focusing on Cost Effectiveness

For nonprofits looking to diversify their revenue streams while maintaining cost-effectiveness, there are several strategies they can employ. Here are a few tips to keep in mind:

- **Prioritize spending:** It's important to regularly evaluate spending and prioritize what's most important to the organization. Make sure all spending aligns with the organization's mission and goals and eliminate what's not necessary. Don't forget reviewing both your ROM and ROI.

- **Look for low-cost revenue options:** While diversifying revenue streams, it's important to keep an eye out for low-cost options that can bring in significant revenue. For example, a membership organization might consider offering hands-on online courses or webinars to its members, which can be cost-effective to produce and deliver.

- **Automate wherever possible:** Utilizing technology to automate tasks can help reduce costs and streamline operations. For example, automating membership management processes can help free up staff time for more critical tasks.

- **Collaborate with other organizations:** Look for opportunities to collaborate with other nonprofits or businesses to share resources and reduce costs. Joint events or shared administrative services are just a couple examples of ways to collaborate.
- **Negotiate with suppliers:** Regularly negotiate with suppliers to reduce costs on products and services. Nonprofits can often get better deals by negotiating as a group, if possible.
- **Continuously evaluate and adjust:** Regularly evaluate the organization's spending and revenue streams to ensure they're aligned with the organization's mission and goals. Make adjustments as needed to optimize cost-effectiveness.

For example, a nonprofit that provides educational resources and support to underprivileged youth can use these strategies to optimize cost-effectiveness and achieve its mission.

To streamline its operations, the organization has automated its membership management processes, freeing up staff time for more critical tasks. It has also collaborated with other nonprofits to share resources, such as hosting joint events and sharing administrative services. Additionally, the organization has regularly negotiated with suppliers to reduce costs on necessary products and services.

Finally, the organization continuously evaluates and adjusts its spending and revenue streams to ensure that they align with its mission and goals. By utilizing these strategies, the nonprofit organization has been able to optimize its cost-effectiveness and achieve its mission of providing educational resources and support to underprivileged youth.

Investing in Technology

In the world of nonprofits, resources are often scarce and budgets are tight, which is why it's common to see organizations underinvest in technology. On average, large nonprofits spend a paltry 2–4% of their overall budget on technology. However, in today's fast-paced and increasingly digital world, technology has the potential to be a game-changer for nonprofits, and that spending should be at least three-fold.

Here are some reasons why investing in technology is so important:

- **Efficiency:** By automating repetitive tasks and streamlining processes, technology can help nonprofits save time and increase efficiency. This, in turn, frees up resources for more impactful activities.
- **Data management:** With the help of technology, nonprofits can better manage and analyze their data, making informed decisions based on up-to-date information.
- **Increased engagement:** Technology can help nonprofits engage with their members, donors, and other stakeholders in new and innovative ways, whether it's through social media, email marketing, or online events.
- **Fundraising:** Technology can play a significant role in fundraising efforts, helping organizations reach a wider audience, process donations more efficiently, and measure the success of their efforts.

- **Collaboration:** Technology can help nonprofits collaborate more effectively with their stakeholders, including staff, volunteers, members, board members, and supporters.

While it may seem daunting to invest in technology, the benefits are well worth it. By utilizing technology, nonprofits can not only increase efficiency and effectiveness, but also achieve their mission in new and innovative ways.

Foster a Culture of Transparency and Accountability

The value of transparency and accountability in the nonprofit sector cannot be overstated. These core values provide a foundation of trust and confidence that are essential for growth and long-term sustainability.

A culture of transparency and accountability allows organizations to build stronger relationships with their members, donors, and other stakeholders. When they are kept informed about how their dues and contributions are being used, they are more likely to feel invested in the organization and its mission. This can lead to increased loyalty and engagement.

Moreover, transparency and accountability can help organizations make better use of their resources. When everyone has a clear understanding of the organization's financial situation and priorities, they can work together to identify areas for improvement and make informed decisions about where to allocate resources. This can help organizations avoid waste and ensure that every dollar is being used effectively to advance the organization's mission.

A culture of transparency and accountability can be an important tool for risk management. When organizations are open and transparent about their operations and finances, they are less likely to be caught off guard by unexpected challenges or controversies.

Having a reputation for transparency and accountability can be crucial for nonprofits in maintaining trust, especially during times of challenge. This trust can lead to loyalty, which is invaluable. Thus, transparency and accountability are vital for nonprofits aiming to diversify their revenue streams and achieve sustainable growth. By prioritizing these values, organizations can build stronger relationships with stakeholders, optimize their use of resources, and mitigate risks effectively. In short, fostering a culture of transparency and accountability is essential for nonprofits looking to succeed in today's challenging environment.

Chapter Six: Planning Succession

In order for a nonprofit organization to ensure a smooth transition in leadership, effective succession planning is crucial. This requires recognizing the key positions that are essential to the organization's success and prioritizing them in the planning process.

While all positions play an important role, the positions of chair, vice-chair, treasurer, and secretary are critical due to their responsibility for overseeing governance and financial management. Additionally, committee chairs should also be identified as they contribute significantly to the organization's success.

(It is important to note that in many nonprofit organizations, the positions referred to as *chair* and *vice-chair* in this section may also be referred to as *president* and *vice-president*.)

In a nonprofit organization, the chair and vice-chair hold the primary responsibility of providing leadership and direction to the board, while the treasurer oversees the organization's finances and collaborates with the CEO to build financial sustainability. The secretary plays a crucial role in ensuring compliance with legal requirements and maintaining accurate records. However, it's important to note that in the presence of a professional staff team, many of the administrative functions will be delegated to the staff team while the volunteer leaders serve in more of an oversight role. This underscores the importance of having a well-functioning staff team that is capable of carrying out the day-to-day operations of the organization, freeing up the volunteer leaders to focus on long-term planning and strategic decision-making.

Identifying potential successors, developing leadership training programs, and establishing a clear timeline for leadership transitions are all essential steps in the succession planning process.

By focusing on these critical positions, nonprofit organizations can guarantee continuity of leadership and maintain their mission-driven work. This involves prioritizing the development of potential successors, including cultivating a diverse and inclusive pool of candidates. Continual evaluation and improvement of the succession plan is also essential, as is preparing for emergency succession situations and addressing any challenges and pitfalls that may arise.

Effective succession planning requires a proactive approach to identifying key positions within an organization and developing a comprehensive plan that prioritizes the organization's long-term success. By doing so, nonprofit organizations can ensure a smooth transition in leadership and maintain their important work towards achieving their mission.

Conducting a Board Skills Assessment

A crucial step in effective succession planning for nonprofit boards is conducting a board skills assessment. This assessment can help identify any gaps in skills or experience on the board and guide the recruitment and development of new board members. By understanding the strengths and weaknesses of the current board, the organization can create a more diverse and effective board that is better equipped to address the challenges facing the nonprofit.

Here's how to implement a board skills assessment:

- **Define the skills and experiences required**: Begin by creating a list of skills and experiences that are essential for the board to effectively carry out the organization's mission. This could include expertise in fundraising, financial management, legal compliance, marketing, or other relevant areas.

- **Evaluate current board members**: Once the necessary skills have been identified, evaluate the current board members' skills and experience against the defined list. This can be done through self-assessment surveys, interviews, or evaluations by other board members or staff.

- **Identify gaps**: Identify any gaps in the current board's skills and experience compared to the defined list. This will help provide an understanding of which areas need to be prioritized in the recruitment of new board members.

- **Recruit new board members**: Use the information from the assessment to prioritize recruitment efforts and identify potential new board members who possess the necessary skills and experience to fill the gaps. Consider seeking out individuals who bring diversity of thought, experience, and perspectives to the board.

- **Develop current board members**: In addition to recruiting new board members, the assessment can guide the development of current board members. Offer training or professional development opportunities to help fill gaps and enhance the board's overall effectiveness.

- **Continually reassess**: Regularly reassess the board's skills and experience to ensure that the board remains effective and aligned with its mission and goals. Conducting a skills assessment on a regular basis will help ensure that the board remains diverse, effective, and able to respond to changing needs and challenges.

Creating a Succession Plan Timeline

A successful succession plan for nonprofit boards requires a timeline that outlines the key steps and milestones in the process. This timeline should include regular reviews and a clear plan of action for when key positions become vacant. The timeline should also consider the needs of the organization and the availability of potential candidates, ensuring that the organization is not left without key leadership positions for an extended period of time.

Here are some tips for developing a successful succession plan:

- **Establish a timeline:** Create a timeline that outlines the key steps and milestones in the succession planning process. This timeline should include regular reviews of the plan and a clear plan of action for when key positions become vacant.
- **Prioritize key positions:** Identify the critical positions that are essential to the organization's success and prioritize them in the planning process. As mentioned previously, these roles

usually encompass the chairperson, vice-chair, treasurer, secretary, and also committee chairs.

- **Consider organizational needs:** Consider the needs of the organization and the availability of potential candidates when developing the succession plan. This will ensure that the organization is not left without key leadership positions for an extended period of time.

- **Develop potential candidates:** Identify potential candidates for key positions and develop leadership training programs to prepare them for leadership roles. This can involve providing mentorship, coaching, and professional development opportunities.

- **Communicate the plan:** Ensure that the succession plan is communicated effectively to all board members, staff, and stakeholders. This will help to ensure that everyone understands the plan and is prepared for transitions in leadership.

Evaluating and Improving the Succession Plan

A successful succession plan is not a one-time event, but rather an ongoing process that requires continual evaluation and improvement. It is essential that the organization regularly reviews its plan to ensure that it is aligned with its mission, vision, and goals. This includes identifying areas for improvement and making changes as necessary to ensure that the plan remains effective and relevant over time.

In addition to regular evaluation, the organization should also incorporate a culture of continuous improvement in the succession planning process. This means consistently seeking out new ways to make the plan more efficient and effective. This can include exploring new methods for identifying potential candidates or improving the training and development of new board members.

By committing to ongoing evaluation and improvement, the organization can ensure that its succession plan remains relevant and effective in meeting evolving needs.

Importance of Staff Team Succession

Succession planning is not just limited to volunteer positions. It is equally important for nonprofit organizations to have a plan in place for the staff team. While it is normally the responsibility of the paid CEO to develop the staff succession plan, it should be reviewed by the board. The departure of key staff members can have a significant impact on an organization's ability to fulfill its mission and maintain its operations.

It is essential for nonprofits to prioritize succession planning for staff members and develop a comprehensive plan that identifies critical positions and potential successors. This requires regularly evaluating the skills and experience of staff members and identifying areas for growth and development.

Succession planning for staff members also involves creating a culture of learning and development that encourages staff members to develop their skills and take on new challenges. Nonprofits should prioritize professional development opportunities, mentorship programs, and career advancement pathways for staff members.

By prioritizing succession planning for both volunteer and staff positions, nonprofit organizations can ensure continuity of leadership and maintain their important work towards achieving their mission. This involves being proactive in identifying key positions and potential successors, developing a comprehensive plan, and continually evaluating and improving the plan as needed.

Preparing for Emergency Succession Situations

While succession planning is typically focused on planned transitions in leadership, it is also important for nonprofit boards to be prepared for emergency succession situations. This includes developing a plan of action in the event of an unexpected vacancy in a key leadership position, such as the chair or the paid CEO position. By having a plan in place, the organization can ensure that it is able to maintain stability and continuity in the face of unexpected challenges.

Integrating emergency succession planning into a nonprofit's overall succession plan requires taking specific steps to prepare for unexpected vacancies in key leadership positions. Firstly, the organization should identify which positions are critical and should have an emergency succession plan in place. These positions typically include the chair, paid CEO, and other key leadership roles that are vital to the organization's success.

Once these positions have been identified, the organization should develop a clear and comprehensive plan of action for how to handle an unexpected vacancy. This plan should include identifying potential interim leaders who can step in to fill the position until a permanent replacement can be found.

The organization should also establish a process for identifying and recruiting qualified candidates, which may involve reaching out to external networks and conducting targeted outreach to individuals with the necessary skills and experience.

In addition to these specific steps, the emergency succession plan should be regularly reviewed and updated to ensure that it remains relevant and effective. This includes evaluating the plan's effectiveness in responding to past emergency situations and making any necessary changes to improve the organization's preparedness for future emergencies.

By integrating emergency succession planning into the overall succession plan, nonprofit organizations can ensure that they are well-prepared to handle unexpected vacancies and maintain continuity in key leadership positions. This can help to mitigate potential disruptions and ensure that the organization is able to continue its important work without interruption.

Chapter Seven: Managing Conflicts

Conflict is an inevitable part of serving on a nonprofit board, but it is important for board members to understand the different types of conflicts that can arise and how to manage them effectively.

Interpersonal conflicts are one of the most common types of conflicts that can arise. These conflicts may be caused by differences in communication styles, personality clashes, or perceived slights. Interpersonal conflicts can often be resolved through open communication, active listening, and a willingness to compromise.

Disagreements over strategic direction or decision-making are another common source of conflict. These conflicts may arise when board members have different opinions about the organization's priorities or the best course of action for achieving its mission. To manage these conflicts effectively, it is important for board members to engage in open and honest discussions about their perspectives and to work together to find common ground.

Conflicts between the board and the paid CEO can also arise on a nonprofit board. These conflicts may be caused by disagreements over the division of responsibilities, differences in communication styles, or misunderstandings about the organization's priorities. To manage these conflicts effectively, it is important for the board to establish clear lines of communication with the CEO to work together to identify and address any issues that may be contributing to the conflict, while keeping the strategic plan front and center.

Causes of Conflicts

Previously, we identified the different types of conflict that can arise on a nonprofit board. However, understanding the underlying causes of these conflicts can be equally important in effectively managing them.

One common cause of conflict is differences in personality or communication styles among board members. For example, if one board member prefers direct communication while another prefers a more indirect approach, this can lead to misunderstandings and tension. Similarly, if some board members are more assertive while others are more reserved, this can also create conflict when it comes to decision-making and strategy.

Power imbalances can also be a cause of conflict on nonprofit boards. For example, if the board chair or CEO has significantly more power or influence than other board members, this can create resentment and a feeling of marginalization among those who feel less powerful. Similarly, if certain board members have significant financial or other resources at their disposal, this can also create a power dynamic that can lead to conflict.

Unclear roles and responsibilities can also contribute to conflict. If board members are unsure about their specific roles or the boundaries of their authority, this can lead to confusion and disagreements over decision-making.

Finally, disagreements over priorities or values can also be a cause of conflict. For example, if some board members prioritize fundraising while others prioritize programmatic outcomes, this can create tension and disagreements over the best course of action for the organization.

By identifying the underlying causes of conflict on nonprofit boards, board members and staff can work proactively to prevent conflicts from arising and address them effectively when they do occur.

Strategies for Preventing Conflict

Preventing conflict on a nonprofit board is essential for creating a positive and productive work environment.

One strategy is to establish clear expectations and guidelines for communication, decision-making, and conflict resolution. This can include setting ground rules for board meetings, such as limiting interruptions, active listening, and maintaining a respectful tone. By establishing these guidelines, board members can work together more effectively and avoid misunderstandings that can lead to conflict.

Another strategy is to encourage open and honest communication between board members. This can be done by creating opportunities to share their perspectives and ideas in a safe and non-judgmental environment. For example, regular check-ins or feedback sessions can help board members to address issues before they escalate into conflict.

In addition, building a culture of trust and respect among board members can help to prevent conflict. This can include recognizing and valuing the diverse perspectives and experiences of each member and creating a sense of shared ownership and responsibility for the success of the organization.

Strategies for Managing Conflict

When it comes to managing conflicts effectively, it is important to address them promptly and directly. The longer conflicts are left unaddressed, the more they can fester and escalate, potentially causing more damage to relationships and the organization as a whole. When a conflict arises, it is best to address it as soon as possible and in a private setting where all parties involved can speak openly and honestly.

One effective strategy for managing conflict is to establish clear protocols for conflict resolution. This can include setting guidelines for communication, outlining specific steps for addressing conflicts, and identifying individuals or resources that can be called upon to mediate or facilitate discussions.

By having a clear and consistent process for handling conflicts, board members can feel more confident in addressing issues as they arise and be better equipped to work towards a positive resolution.

Here are the top seven resolution protocols that can be followed:

1. **Identify the issue:** The first step in resolving a conflict is to identify the issue at hand. This may involve bringing in an outside mediator or facilitator to help parties identify the root cause of the conflict.
2. **Gather information:** Once the issue has been identified; it is important to gather as much information as possible about the conflict. This may involve talking to all parties involved,

reviewing relevant documents or policies, and gathering feedback from stakeholders.

3. **Identify possible solutions:** Based on the information gathered, parties should work together to identify possible solutions to the conflict. This may involve brainstorming, discussing various options, and identifying common ground.

4. **Evaluate potential solutions:** Once possible solutions have been identified, parties should evaluate and weigh the pros and cons of each option.

5. **Agree on a solution:** After evaluating potential solutions, parties should work together to agree on a solution that meets the needs of all stakeholders.

6. **Implement the solution:** Once a solution has been agreed upon, it is important to implement it in a timely and effective manner. This may involve assigning specific tasks or responsibilities to individual parties.

7. **Evaluate the outcome:** After the solution has been implemented, it is important to evaluate the outcome and determine whether the conflict has been fully resolved. If not, parties

may need to revisit the issue and continue the conflict resolution process.

In some cases, no matter what the protocol, it may be helpful to bring in an outside mediator or facilitator to assist with conflict resolution. This can be particularly beneficial when conflicts are especially complex or involve deeply ingrained disagreements. A neutral third party can help to facilitate productive discussions and identify common ground, ultimately helping to find a resolution that satisfies all parties involved.

10 Conflicts Nonprofits Face and How to Address Them

As we detailed earlier, conflicts can arise on nonprofit boards for a variety of reasons, ranging from power struggles to personality clashes. Resolving these conflicts is essential for maintaining a functional and effective board that can successfully lead the organization towards its mission. In this top ten list, we will explore some of the most common conflicts that arise on nonprofit boards and provide solutions for addressing them. By proactively addressing these conflicts, nonprofit boards can create a more productive and harmonious environment that supports the growth and success of the organization.

#1 Conflict of Interest: A conflict of interest occurs when board members have personal interests that may interfere with their ability to make unbiased decisions for the organization.

Solution: Adopt and strictly enforce a conflict of interest policy that requires board members to disclose any potential conflicts and recuse themselves from decision-making processes where they may have a conflict of interest.

#2 Personality Clashes: Differences in personalities, communication styles, and personal agendas can lead to misunderstandings, tension, and conflict among board members.

Solution: Encourage open communication and respect among board members, establish clear expectations for behavior and conduct, and address conflicts as soon as they arise by promoting active listening, mutual understanding, and collaborative problem-solving.

#3 **Power Struggles**: Power struggles occur when board members compete for control or influence over the organization, often leading to division and dysfunction.

Solution: Establish clear lines of authority and decision-making processes, delegate responsibilities and tasks based on each member's strengths, and foster a culture of trust and respect.

#4 **Lack of Clarity or Vision**: Conflicts can arise when there is a lack of clarity or alignment around the organization's mission, goals, or strategies.

Solution: Develop a clear and shared vision for the organization, set measurable goals and objectives, and regularly review and adjust the strategic plan as needed.

#5 **Micromanagement**: Board members may micromanage staff or operations, leading to inefficiency, frustration, and conflict.

Solution: Define clear roles and responsibilities for the board and staff, establish performance metrics and accountability measures, and encourage board members to focus on strategic oversight rather than day-to-day operations.

#6 **Lack of Engagement**: Disengaged board members can create a sense of apathy and disunity, leading to a lack of progress or momentum.

Solution: Foster a culture of engagement and participation, establish regular meeting schedules and agendas, and provide opportunities for board members to contribute their expertise and perspectives.

#7 **Financial Disagreements**: Financial disagreements can occur when there is a lack of transparency or accountability around the organization's finances, or when board members have different priorities or goals for the use of funds.

Solution: Establish clear financial policies and procedures, ensure regular financial reporting and audits, and engage in open and honest communication around financial decisions and priorities.

#8 Governance Issues: Governance issues can arise when there is a lack of clarity or understanding around the roles and responsibilities of the board, or when there are conflicts over decision-making processes.

Solution: Define clear governance structures and processes, establish regular performance evaluations and assessments, and provide ongoing training and support for board members.

#9 Resistance to Change: Resistance to change can occur when board members are reluctant to adopt new ideas or approaches, leading to stagnation and missed opportunities.

Solution: Encourage innovation and creativity, establish a culture of continuous learning and improvement, and provide opportunities for board members to explore new ideas and approaches.

#10 **Lack of Communication**: Lack of communication among board members can lead to misunderstandings, misaligned expectations, and conflict.

Solution: Establish clear communication channels and protocols, encourage open and transparent communication, and provide opportunities for regular check-ins and updates. Implement regular board meetings and establish a culture of active listening, mutual understanding, and collaborative problem-solving.

Unavoidable Conflicts at Board Meetings

Sometimes conflicts can't be avoided during a board meeting. When a conflict arises during a board meeting, it's important to have strategies in place to address it and redirect the conversation to a productive outcome. The worst thing that can happen is a conflict escalates out of control.

One effective strategy is to have a pre-established process for managing conflicts during meetings, such as a "time out" or "cooling off" period where participants can take a break and collect their thoughts. This can help prevent conflicts from escalating and provide an opportunity for individuals to reflect on their emotions and feelings. Sometimes taking a 15-minute break is all that is needed to get the meeting back on track.

Given the nature of virtual meetings, another effective strategy could be to incorporate technology tools into board meetings, such as real-time polling or anonymous feedback platforms, which can help to identify areas of disagreement or tension before they become full-blown conflicts. This allows the board to proactively address issues and work towards a resolution, rather than letting conflicts fester and worsen over time.

It can also be helpful to establish ground rules for communication during meetings, such as listening actively and respectfully to other perspectives, refraining from personal attacks or disrespectful language, and focusing on the issue at hand rather than personal agendas or biases.

If the conflict cannot be resolved during the meeting, it may be necessary to table the discussion for a later time when all parties involved can approach the issue with a cooler head and more rational perspective.

In order to manage conflicts effectively, it is important to recognize unproductive conflicts and intervene in a timely manner to redirect the discussion to a more appropriate time or setting. By doing so, the board can avoid getting bogged down in unproductive debates and instead focus on productive and constructive dialogue that leads to meaningful outcomes.

Board Dysfunction

Board dysfunction can pose a significant obstacle to effectively resolving conflicts as it may render typical resolution strategies ineffective or unavailable. Dysfunctional board behavior can include things like lack of transparency, failure to communicate effectively, and inability to work collaboratively. These issues can create an environment where conflicts are more likely to occur and are less likely to be resolved in a productive way.

When there is dysfunction within a board, conflicts may be more likely to escalate or persist, as there may be underlying issues that are not being addressed. For example, if there is a power struggle among board members, this may make it difficult to resolve conflicts that arise because individuals may be more focused on asserting their own power than finding a mutually beneficial solution.

It is important to address board dysfunction proactively, before conflicts arise. As discussed, this includes things like establishing clear expectations for board behavior and communication, providing training and resources for board members, and taking steps to foster a positive and collaborative board culture.

Nonprofit boards can experience dysfunction in various forms, from disagreements on strategic direction to major conflicts of interest involving board members, which can significantly hinder their effectiveness in fulfilling the organization's mission. To illustrate one example of such dysfunction, let's explore a hypothetical scenario involving a major conflict of interest and what we can learn from it.

Imagine a nonprofit organization's board of directors is experiencing dysfunction due to a major conflict of interest involving one of its members. The member in question is also the CEO of a company that the organization regularly does business with, creating a clear conflict of interest. The board member in question is using their influence on the board to steer business towards their own company, rather than what is in the best interest of the organization.

To resolve this issue in a professional way, the board chair can initiate a private discussion with the conflicted board member to express concerns about their behavior and to explain the ethical and legal implications of a conflict of interest. The chair can then suggest bringing in an independent ethics consultant to provide guidance on best practices and to lead a board workshop focused on the topic.

If the board member refuses to acknowledge or address the conflict of interest, the chair can suggest they step down from the board to avoid any further damage to the organization's reputation. Alternatively, if the board member is willing to address the conflict, the board can establish a subcommittee to review all contracts and business dealings with the conflicted board member's company to ensure they are in line with ethical standards and best practices.

By addressing the conflict of interest head-on and seeking outside expertise, the board can work towards maintaining the organization's integrity and reputation while fulfilling its mission.

Moving Forward After Conflict

Moving forward as a board after a conflict has been resolved can be a challenging process, but it is also an opportunity for growth and learning. It is important to take time to reflect on the lessons learned from the conflict and identify areas for improvement. This can involve reviewing communication protocols, decision-making processes, and conflict resolution strategies to determine what worked well and what can be improved upon in the future.

Establishing new norms or processes can be a key part of moving forward as a board. This may involve setting clear expectations for communication and behavior, establishing regular check-ins to ensure that conflicts are addressed in a timely manner, or creating a system for providing feedback and constructive criticism.

Finally, reaffirming the board's commitment to the organization's mission and values can help to restore trust and rebuild relationships among board members. This may involve revisiting the organization's strategic plan or mission statement and identifying specific actions that the board can take to demonstrate its commitment to these values.

Moving forward after a conflict requires a willingness to learn from past mistakes, a commitment to open communication and collaboration, and a shared sense of purpose and commitment to the organization's mission and goals.

As previously discussed, nonprofit boards can experience dysfunction in various forms, from disagreements on strategic direction to major conflicts of interest involving board members, which can significantly hinder their effectiveness in fulfilling the organization's mission. By approaching conflicts with a focus on cooperation and collaboration, nonprofit boards can ensure that they are able to manage conflicts effectively and maintain positive relationships among board members and stakeholders. However, there may be situations where conflicts cannot be resolved through discussion and more drastic actions, such as removing board members, suspending them from their duties, or seeking mediation or arbitration, are necessary to protect the organization's interests.

Chapter Eight: Building a High-Performing Team

The foundation of a successful nonprofit organization is a strong, high-performing paid professional staff team. A team that is diverse, collaborative, and engaged in the mission is essential for achieving both short-term and long-term goals. Building a great team requires focus and investment in a number of key areas, from setting clear goals and expectations to fostering a positive and inclusive culture.

In this section, we will delve into the crucial elements of creating a successful and high-performing team and offer actionable insights to implement these principles in your organization.

Communication

Communication stands as the foremost and essential element that forms the bedrock of any team's success. Without it, no team can thrive. Effective communication acts as a crucial cornerstone for teams that strive for excellence, enabling members to gain insight into each other's perspectives, align their expectations, and establish a collaborative culture built on trust.

To ensure powerful communication within your nonprofit team, consider implementing the following strategies:

- **Establish clear communication channels and protocols:** This might include regular team meetings, weekly check-ins, or designated channels for asking questions and providing updates.
- **Encourage open and honest communication:** Create a safe space for team members to share their thoughts and ideas, and actively listen to feedback and suggestions.
- **Foster transparency:** Ensure that everyone on the team has access to the same information and encourage team members to share their opinions and ask questions.
- **Practice active listening:** Pay attention to what team members are saying and show that you value their input by responding thoughtfully and respectfully.

- **Manage conflict constructively:** When disagreements arise, address them head-on and work towards finding a mutually beneficial resolution.

Collaboration

In the world of high-performing teams, collaboration is a required characteristic in delivering the highest level of service to an organization's members and stakeholders. The ability for team members to work together effectively and efficiently, combining their unique skills, perspectives, and experiences, is what sets a top-performing team apart from the rest.

But how do we foster an environment of collaboration within our teams? I would argue that it all starts with understanding the psychology of human behavior.

To build collaboration in a high-performing team, we must first understand what drives people to work together. It's not just about shared goals or the desire to succeed. It's about the underlying factors that influence how people interact, how they approach problems, and how they make decisions. This understanding can inform how we build and lead teams, creating an environment that encourages and facilitates collaboration.

One of the key ways to foster collaboration is to create an atmosphere of trust. This trust should be built through clear communication, transparency, and a shared sense of purpose. Teams that trust each other are more likely to work together effectively and make decisions that are in the best interest of the group.

Another important factor in building collaboration is the creation of a shared vision. Teams that have a common goal are more likely to work together towards that goal. This vision should be communicated clearly and often, ensuring that everyone understands what they are working towards and how their contributions fit into the bigger picture.

The "x-factor" of a high-performing collaborative team can be described as the intangible, yet essential quality that sets it apart and drives its success. It could be shared vision and values, the sense of camaraderie and trust among members, or the collective mindset and approach to problem-solving. This elusive quality is what creates a synergistic dynamic, allowing them to achieve more together than they would individually. Finding and nurturing the x-factor is crucial in building a high-performing, collaborative team that can drive results and change.

Finally, it's important to recognize and value the unique strengths and skills of each team member. When each member feels valued and their contributions are recognized, they are more likely to be invested in the success of the team and more willing to collaborate and work together.

Here are a few activities that can help foster trust among team members:

- **Get to know each other:** Encourage them to share their backgrounds, experiences, and personal interests. This helps to build a deeper understanding and connection.
- **Set common goals:** Having a clear and shared understanding of what the team is working towards helps to build trust and accountability.

- **Encourage open communication:** Encourage them to express their thoughts, ideas, and concerns freely. This helps to create a culture of transparency and fosters an environment of trust.

- **Lead by example:** The team leader should model the behavior they wish to see. By being trustworthy, transparent, and accountable, the leader can help build trust among team members.

- **Establish clear processes and expectations:** Establishing clear and well-defined processes for decision-making, communication, and project management can help to build trust and accountability.

Building collaboration requires an intentional approach, but the benefits are well worth the effort. Teams that work together effectively are more likely to achieve their goals and create a positive impact in their organizations and communities.

Trust

Building and maintaining trust in a high-performing team is not just about adhering to principles and ethical behavior; it's about creating a shared sense of purpose and understanding. It's about inspiring each other to work together toward a common goal and fostering a culture of mutual respect and vulnerability.

Just as Simon Sinek, author of *Start with Why*, says, "People don't buy what you do, they buy why you do it."

By first understanding each other's motivations, values, and aspirations, team members can build a foundation of trust that enables them to overcome obstacles and achieve their goals together. This foundation of trust allows them to be open and transparent with one another, to admit when they need help or guidance, and to collaborate effectively, even in the face of disagreement or adversity.

If trust is broken in a high-performing team, it's important to address the issue head-on and find a solution that restores trust. This can involve several steps, including:

- **Identifying the root cause of the trust breakdown:** Understanding the reasons behind the breakdown in trust can help you address the issue effectively.

- **Encourage open and honest communication:** Encourage all team members to express their feelings and concerns in a non-confrontational manner.

- **Establish a plan of action:** Work together to establish a plan of action that addresses the issue and restores trust.

- **Implement the plan:** Take action to implement the plan and follow through on commitments.

- **Continuously monitor the situation:** Check in regularly to see if the trust has been restored and if not, continue to take steps to address the issue.

- **Foster a culture of trust:** Once it has been restored, work to maintain it by promoting transparency, open communication, and a culture of mutual respect and understanding.

By following these steps, you can help restore trust and build a high-performing team that is capable of collaborating effectively and achieving success.

Leadership

Great leaders throughout history have demonstrated qualities such as empathy, resilience, and the ability to inspire and empower others. They exhibit decisive and visionary leadership, effortlessly inspiring trust and loyalty among those they lead. Their unwavering determination and unique perspective pave the way for others to follow with conviction.

To build leadership in a high-performing team, it's important to start by identifying and nurturing these qualities in individuals, and then encouraging them to take on leadership roles. This can include offering training and development opportunities, providing feedback and support, and recognizing and rewarding those who demonstrate strong leadership skills.

Additionally, it's important to create an environment in which leadership is valued and respected, and where everyone is encouraged to step up and contribute in their own unique way.

Ultimately, strong leadership is a combination of having the right people in place, providing the tools and resources they need to succeed, and creating a culture that values and supports excellence in leadership.

Visionary leaders have the power to shape the course of history, leaving a lasting impact on the world. From Martin Luther King Jr to Gandhi, these figures inspire us with their unwavering dedication to a cause and their exceptional leadership skills. Let us delve into their stories and uncover the secrets to their success.

Martin Luther King Jr.

Martin Luther King Jr. was a prominent figure in the Civil Rights Movement and one of the most influential leaders in modern American history. He is widely known for his use of nonviolent resistance and civil disobedience in the pursuit of equal rights for African Americans. He inspired a nation with his charismatic speeches, unwavering determination, and relentless pursuit of justice.

From King's leadership, we can learn several valuable lessons. Firstly, King believed in the power of a clear vision and strong values. He had a vivid vision of an America where all people, regardless of race, were treated with dignity and respect. He communicated this vision with unwavering passion and clarity, and inspired millions to join his cause.

Another important lesson from King's leadership is the importance of courage and perseverance. He faced significant opposition and adversity in his efforts, but he never lost faith in his cause and never backed down from what he believed was right. He demonstrated that true leadership requires the courage to stand up for what is right, even in the face of overwhelming opposition.

King also showed us the importance of teamwork and collaboration. He recognized the power of bringing people together to achieve a common goal and worked tirelessly to build a coalition of diverse groups to support the Civil Rights Movement. He understood that great leadership requires the ability to bring people together and to work with others towards a shared vision.

Finally, King's legacy teaches us the importance of self-reflection and personal growth. He was a man of deep faith and spirituality, and he recognized the importance of continually working on himself to become the best leader he could be. He believed in the power of love and compassion, and he demonstrated that great leaders are those who are not afraid to lead with their hearts as well as their heads.

Mahatma Gandhi

Mahatma Gandhi is known for his remarkable leadership and the impact he made on Indian independence and the world at large. He was a visionary who inspired countless people through his nonviolent resistance and self-determination movement.

Gandhi's leadership style was rooted in humility, courage, and unwavering commitment to his beliefs. He believed in the power of collective action and always sought to bring people together in a shared mission.

He was a master of communication and was able to articulate his ideas in a way that motivated and inspired others to take action. Gandhi's leadership lessons are relevant today, and they demonstrate the power of nonviolence, perseverance, and moral leadership in creating lasting change.

Mother Teresa

Mother Teresa, a Nobel Peace Prize winner, is known for her selfless and compassionate leadership in serving the poor and sick. She embodied the ideals of kindness, humility, and love in her work, inspiring countless people to follow in her footsteps.

Through her leadership, she taught the importance of putting others before oneself and dedicating one's life to serving those in need. She also demonstrated the power of faith in guiding and sustaining one's leadership, as her strong spiritual beliefs motivated her to help those in need.

Mother Teresa's leadership serves as a shining example of how one person can make a profound impact on the world through their unwavering dedication to serving others.

Despite their vastly different backgrounds and circumstances, great leaders such as Martin Luther King Jr., Gandhi, and Mother Teresa share several key characteristics that made them effective leaders. Some of these common traits include: a strong sense of purpose and vision, the ability to inspire and empower others, a deep understanding of human nature, the capacity for self-reflection and self-improvement, the ability to communicate effectively, and a willingness to take bold action to achieve their goals. Ultimately, what all of these leaders have in common is the ability to bring people together to achieve something greater than themselves, and to inspire others to work towards a common goal.

Humility lies at the heart of great leadership, elevating the leader to inspire and guide with grace and compassion. Humility is important in the leadership of a nonprofit because it allows leaders to listen to their team, stakeholders, and community members, and to consider the perspectives and needs of those they serve. A humble leader is more approachable, open-minded, and empathetic, which fosters a positive work environment and promotes trust and cooperation.

Additionally, humility helps leaders stay grounded and focused on the mission and goals of the organization, rather than personal egos or agendas. By demonstrating humility, leaders can effectively inspire and guide their teams towards a common goal and drive meaningful change in their communities.

Effective and intuitive leaders understand that not everyone is cut out for a leadership role. While some individuals have the skills, drive, and charisma to lead, others may be better suited for supporting roles. Recognizing this is a crucial aspect of good leadership, as it enables leaders to allocate resources and responsibilities in a way that is most effective and fulfilling for each individual.

Great leaders have the ability to assess the strengths and weaknesses of their team members, and they are able to place them in roles that best utilize their skills and align with their personal goals and aspirations. By doing so, leaders are able to create a high-performing team where each person feels valued and fulfilled, and where everyone is able to contribute to the collective success of the organization. Ultimately, this allows for a more harmonious and productive work environment, where everyone is working towards a common goal and contributing to the greater good.

Skills and Expertise

One famous quote from Jim Collins' book *Good to Great* regarding building a talented team is, "Get the right people on the bus, the wrong people off the bus, and the right people in the right seats."

This quote emphasizes the importance of having the right team members and placing them in roles that align with their strengths and skills.

A team comprised of individuals with diverse skills and expertise is more adaptive, resilient, and capable of creating sustained impact. In short, skills and expertise are essential components in building a powerful, high-performing team that can achieve great things.

Building a successful and high-performing team is like piecing together a complex puzzle. Each member brings their unique skills and expertise to the table, fitting precisely into the larger picture. When all the pieces come together, the result is a dynamic group that can approach challenges from multiple angles and generate innovative solutions. With a diversity of perspectives, the team is equipped to tackle even the most daunting tasks with confidence and poise. This is the essence of great teamwork, where the sum of its parts is greater than any individual contribution.

Just like a puzzle, constructing a team takes patience, planning, and a clear understanding of what each piece brings to the picture. It requires the ability to see beyond the present, envisioning the bigger picture, and aligning the right pieces to bring that vision to life.

As a leader, passively waiting for a top-performing team to materialize by happenstance is not a viable strategy. Achieving a team that excels requires a proactive approach and intentional effort. The process of building, nurturing, and enhancing a team is not one that can be taken lightly, but it is one that holds tremendous reward.

By following a set of specific steps, leaders can lay the foundation for a talented and competent team:

- **Define the skills and expertise needed:** Clearly define what skills and expertise your team needs to perform at a high level. Ensure that it meets the current and expected needs of the organization.
- **Assess the current team:** Take stock of your current team members and their skills, as well as any gaps in expertise.
- **Recruit strategically:** Look for individuals who bring a unique set of skills and expertise to the table.
- **Offer training and development:** Provide ongoing training and development opportunities to help your team members enhance their skills and expertise.
- **Encourage cross-functional collaboration:** Encourage your team members to share their

skills and expertise with one another and facilitate cross-functional collaboration whenever possible.

- **Evaluate performance regularly:** Regularly evaluate your team's performance and identify areas where additional skills or expertise may be needed.

- **Foster a culture of continuous improvement:** Create a culture where your team members are encouraged to continuously improve their skills and expertise, and where they feel supported and valued for doing so.

Building a top-notch team is a journey that requires ongoing effort and attention from the leader. Much like shaping a work of art, crafting a team of high-performing individuals demands a combination of strategy, care, and dedication. With the right steps, however, the result can be nothing short of extraordinary.

By fostering collaboration, trust, and humility among team members, the leader can lay the foundation for a team that is not only expert, but also highly functional. The impact of this extends far beyond its individual members, as it drives the organization towards its goals, delivering exceptional results and contributing to its success.

Location, Location, Location

For any organization, building a high-performing team is essential to achieving its goals and making a positive impact. However, limited resources, competition for talent, and high costs in some geographic locations can make it challenging to build a top-notch team.

Nonprofit organizations, in particular, face unique challenges in building a talented team with limited resources. This is why being flexible in the location of the team is critical to achieving their mission and maximizing their impact. By embracing technology and virtual teams, nonprofits can access a wider pool of talent and reduce costs, while also providing greater flexibility for team members.

The benefits of flexibility in location are numerous. Nonprofits can tap into experts and thought leaders from around the world, rather than just within their geographic location. They can also avoid the challenges of high costs and fierce competition for talent in some areas, making it easier to attract and keep top talent. Furthermore, being flexible in location can also help nonprofits to reduce costs and direct more resources towards their mission.

However, building and managing a virtual team requires specific skills and tools. Nonprofits must develop effective systems and communication protocols to facilitate collaboration, build trust, and ensure that team members are aligned with the organization's mission and goals. They must also provide the necessary resources and support to enable remote workers to succeed.

To recap, being flexible in location is critical to building a high-performing team that can achieve an organization's goals and mission. For nonprofit organizations, this is especially important given their unique challenges in building a talented team with limited resources. By embracing technology and virtual teams, nonprofits can access a wider pool of talent, reduce costs, and provide greater flexibility for team members. However, to make a virtual team work, nonprofits must establish effective systems and communication protocols to ensure that the team is aligned with the organization's values, culture, and mission. With the right approach, nonprofits can build an exceptional team that can make a real difference in the world.

Recognition and Reward

Recognition and reward play a critical role in motivating and retaining top talent in a nonprofit organization. One could argue that effective recognition and reward programs are not just a "nice to have," but a necessary component of building and maintaining a high-performing team.

The key is to implement these programs in a meaningful and personalized way that aligns with the values and goals of the organization. This can be achieved through regular feedback and performance evaluations, setting clear expectations and goals, and offering both monetary and non-monetary incentives that resonate with team members. By doing so, leaders can create a culture of appreciation and encourage continuous improvement and growth within their team.

Implementing these programs in a nonprofit organization requires careful planning and consideration. Here are some steps that can be taken to successfully implement these programs:

1. **Define the goals of the program:** The first step is to determine what the organization hopes to achieve through the recognition and reward program. This could include increasing staff engagement, improving morale, or boosting productivity.

2. **Determine the right mix of recognition and reward:** Decide on the right mix that will work best for the organization. For example, should the program focus more on non-monetary recognition, like public praise, or should it involve more tangible rewards, like bonuses or gifts?

3. **Involve team members in the planning process:** Invite team members to provide input on what types of programs would be meaningful to them. This helps ensure that the program is well-received and that the rewards will have the desired impact.

4. **Create clear guidelines for the program:** Establish clear guidelines for how the program will work, including who is eligible for rewards, how often rewards will be given, and what criteria will be used to determine who is eligible.

5. **Communicate the program to all team members:** Once the program is in place, make sure all team members are aware of how it works, and what they need to do to participate.

6. **Evaluate and refine the program:** Regularly evaluate the success of the program and make any necessary adjustments to ensure that it is meeting its goals and that team members are motivated and engaged.

Recognizing and rewarding your team is a powerful tool to boost morale and motivation, and it doesn't have to be limited to traditional methods. Here are a few examples of unique recognition and reward programs:

- **The "Caught You Doing Good" initiative:** This fosters a culture of positivity and appreciation, where team members have the opportunity to recognize their colleagues for their hard work and dedication. This simple yet effective program encourages team members to look out for each other and to acknowledge the little things that make a big difference in the work environment.

- **Adventure days:** These provide a unique opportunity for team members to bond and collaborate outside of their usual work setting. By participating in outdoor activities and team-building experiences, team members can build trust, improve communication, and strengthen their relationships.

- **Themed parties:** Celebrate milestones and accomplishments in a memorable and exciting way. This allows the team to come together and have some fun, all while recognizing their hard work and achievements. Whether it's a Hawaiian luau, Hollywood Oscars, or a masquerade ball, these events provide an opportunity to let loose and have a good time.

- **Skill development:** Give team members the opportunity to expand their knowledge and skills, setting them up for success both in their current role and in the future. Whether it's attending workshops, conferences, or professional development opportunities, these programs show that the organization values its staff and is committed to their growth and development.

- **"Employee of the Month" awards programs:** This program provides an opportunity for team members to be recognized for their contributions, and encourages healthy competition, motivation, and growth.

- **"Champion of the Quarter" awards:** Recognize team members who demonstrate exceptional leadership, innovation, and impact in their work.

- **Team challenge events:** Foster collaboration and teamwork by having the team compete in friendly challenges such as scavenger hunts, trivia contests, or cooking competitions.

- **Storytelling sessions:** These allow team members to share their personal and professional stories, fostering a deeper connection and understanding among team members.

- **Volunteer day:** Dedicate a day to volunteer work, where the team can give back to their

local community, build camaraderie, and learn
new skills.

- **One-on-one coaching:** This involves providing
team members with the opportunity for
personalized coaching, mentorship, and
feedback from their managers or mentors.

Recognition and reward programs are integral
components of creating a positive, supportive culture
within your nonprofit. Investing in these initiatives
can lead to a range of benefits, including higher job
satisfaction, motivation, and performance from your
team. By acknowledging their hard work and
achievements, you can help retain top talent, foster a
sense of engagement, and support the organization's
mission.

Additionally, these programs serve as motivators and
affirmations, reinforcing a job well done and showing
staff that their contributions are valued. A culture of
appreciation can help retain top-performing staff and
increase satisfaction, ultimately leading to a more
productive and thriving organization.

Work-Life Balance

A harmonious balance between one's personal and professional life is not just desirable; it is crucial for a fulfilling existence. Striving for work-life balance not only benefits the individual, but it also creates a positive work environment and enhances staff satisfaction, leading to increased productivity and reduced burnout. By prioritizing this balance, staff are empowered to bring their best selves to the workplace, perform at their highest levels, and achieve a sense of fulfillment in both their personal and professional lives.

When organizations make a commitment to promoting work-life balance, they send a clear message to their staff that their well-being is valued and appreciated. This creates a supportive and inclusive culture that benefits both the staff and the organization, fostering a sense of loyalty, engagement, and commitment among the workforce.

As a CEO and leader of the professional staff team, it is imperative to lead by example and set the tone for a culture that prioritizes work-life balance within the organization. To achieve this, a CEO should implement the following strategies:

- **Lead from the front:** Model a healthy work-life balance to demonstrate the importance of this issue and set the standard for the team.
- **Clarify expectations:** Clearly communicate the expectations around work-life balance, including work hours, breaks, and paid time off.
- **Foster flexibility:** Encourage flexible work arrangements, such as remote working and flexible schedules, to help staff balance their work and personal lives.
- **Provide resources:** Ensure staff has access to resources that support work-life balance, such as counseling services, wellness programs, and family-friendly benefits.
- **Celebrate success:** Recognize and celebrate those who are making progress in balancing their work and personal lives, to show the organization's commitment to this issue and encourage others to prioritize work-life balance.

- **Regularly evaluate:** Continuously assess the impact of work-life balance initiatives and make changes as needed to ensure the well-being of staff and the success of the organization.

There are a variety of ways that organizations have successfully implemented work-life balance programs. Some examples include:

- **Flexible scheduling:** Offering staff the ability to work outside of traditional office hours—such as remote work or flexible schedules—to help them better manage their work and personal commitments. There has been a real shift to this type of work flexibility and as discussed, virtual work leads to a larger pool of talent.
- **Paid time off:** Providing staff with ample paid time off, such as vacation days, sick days, and personal days, allowing them to take time off as needed to recharge and care for their well-being.
- **Wellness programs:** Implementing wellness programs, such as on-site gym memberships,

stress management classes, or health and wellness workshops.

- **Parental leave:** Offering parental leave—such as maternity, paternity, or adoption leave—to allow staff to take time off to care for a new family member.

- **Employee assistance programs:** Providing staff with access to counseling services, financial advisors, or other support services to help them navigate challenges.

- **Unlimited PTO policy:** This policy allows staff to take as much time off as they need, as long as their work is done and responsibilities are covered.

- **"Work from anywhere" policy:** This policy allows staff the flexibility to work from anywhere, be it from home, a coffee shop, or a different city.

- **Sabbatical leave:** Offering staff the opportunity to take extended time off for personal or professional development.

- **Employee volunteer programs:** Encouraging staff to volunteer for causes they are passionate about, to help them feel fulfilled outside of work.

- **Personal development programs:** Providing resources and opportunities for personal and professional development, such as workshops, courses, and coaching.

These are just a few examples of how organizations can build a culture of work-life balance. By implementing programs that prioritize staff well-being, organizations can create a positive work environment and improve retention.

By creating a work environment that values and supports work-life balance, organizations can attract and retain top talent, increase job satisfaction, and improve overall productivity and efficiency. A positive work-life balance culture is a win-win situation for everyone involved and can lead to a more successful and sustainable organization.

Chapter Nine: Evaluating and Improving Programs and Services

Evaluating and improving programs and services in a nonprofit is crucial to achieving success and creating a positive impact.

At the core of every nonprofit lies a purpose, a cause that drives their mission forward. To fulfill this purpose, it is vital to assess and refine the programs and services offered by the organization. This continuous evaluation process helps to ensure that the organization stays true to its mission, remains relevant, and is effectively serving the needs of its members, constituents, and key stakeholders. By regularly examining and enhancing their offerings, nonprofits can evolve, adapt, and ultimately create a more significant and lasting impact.

Evaluating Membership Association Programs and Services

Evaluating and improving programs and services is particularly important in membership nonprofit organizations as the success of the organization relies on its ability to retain members and attract new ones.

Regular evaluations help ensure that the organization is meeting the needs and expectations of its members, and that its programs and services remain relevant and effective. By continuously improving its offerings, a membership nonprofit organization can demonstrate its commitment to its members and the value of membership. This, in turn, helps to build loyalty and encourages members to remain active and engaged in the organization, contributing to its long-term sustainability and success.

In order for a nonprofit to effectively evaluate and improve its services, it must first establish clear goals and objectives. This allows the organization to measure its progress and determine what areas need improvement.

After setting these goals, the nonprofit can gather data through various methods such as surveys, focus groups, and service evaluations.

This data can then be analyzed to determine areas where the organization is performing well and areas that require improvement. Based on these findings, the nonprofit can create an action plan to address any shortcomings and make changes to its programs and services.

Here are ten actionable steps to guide you through the evaluation and improvement process:

1. Define your objectives and goals for the program or service to be evaluated.
2. Gather relevant data and feedback from members and other stakeholders.
3. Analyze key areas of strength and opportunities for improvement.
4. Compare your program or service to industry best practices.
5. Engage in member feedback and engagement activities.
6. Develop a comprehensive improvement plan with specific goals, strategies, and timelines.
7. Establish metrics for tracking progress and success of the improvement plan.

8. Allocate resources, such as funding and staff, to support the improvement plan.
9. Implement the improvement plan and continuously monitor progress.
10. Evaluate the program or service after a set period of time to measure success and identify areas for ongoing improvement.

Here's an example:

A nonprofit association that represented over 4 million professionals in the healthcare industry faced significant declining membership. After conducting an evaluation of their membership program, they identified several areas for improvement, including a lack of engagement with members, inadequate resources allocated to member benefits, and limited opportunities for networking and professional development.

To address these issues, the nonprofit engaged with members through focus groups, surveys, and one-on-one conversations to gather feedback on their experiences and identify areas for improvement. They also analyzed data on member retention rates, satisfaction levels, and program costs to inform their improvement plan.

Based on this analysis, the nonprofit developed a comprehensive improvement plan that included specific goals, strategies, and timelines for addressing the identified issues. They established metrics for tracking progress and success, such as increased member engagement, higher satisfaction levels, and improved retention rates.

To implement the plan, the nonprofit allocated additional resources, including staff and funding, to support member benefits, networking, and professional development opportunities. They also launched a series of member engagement and outreach activities, such as webinars, conferences, and networking events, to foster stronger connections and relationships among members.

After a set period of time, the nonprofit evaluated the membership program to measure success and identify areas for ongoing improvement. They found that member engagement had increased, satisfaction levels had improved, and retention rates had risen significantly. As a result of these improvements, the nonprofit was able to better deliver on its mission and serve the needs of its members in the healthcare industry.

Evaluating Foundation and Charity Programs and Services

For a nonprofit foundation or charity, the effectiveness and impact of programs and services are essential for fulfilling their mission and providing support to those they serve. One critical aspect of effective nonprofit management is evaluating and continually improving these programs and services.

The following steps provide a roadmap for conducting a thorough program evaluation and making meaningful improvements that drive positive results:

1. Identify the desired outcomes and impact of the foundation's grants and individual contributions.

2. Develop clear metrics and evaluation frameworks to measure progress towards those outcomes.
3. Gather data and feedback from stakeholders, including grantees, beneficiaries, and communities.
4. Conduct a thorough analysis of the program's effectiveness and impact on the community.
5. Engage in regular stakeholder feedback and engagement, including grantees, beneficiaries, and communities.
6. Compare the results of the evaluations to industry standards and best practices.
7. Use the insights from the evaluations to continuously improve programs and services.
8. Create a culture of continuous learning and improvement by regularly assessing the impact of the foundation.
9. Make any necessary adjustments to programs and services to better serve the beneficiaries and communities.
10. Share results and findings with stakeholders, including donors, funders, and grantors, to demonstrate commitment to making a positive impact.

By continuously assessing the effectiveness of its initiatives, it can make informed decisions, adapt to changing circumstances, and refine its approach to achieve maximum impact. This deliberate and proactive approach to evaluation is the key to realizing its full potential, increasing support, and making a lasting impact on the community it serves.

Here's an example of a foundation that has successfully implemented these ten steps:

The foundation in question was focused on providing grants to organizations working to address homelessness in their community. To ensure that their grants were having the desired impact, the foundation implemented a rigorous evaluation framework that incorporated regular stakeholder feedback and engagement.

First, the foundation identified the desired outcomes and impact of their grants, including reducing the number of people experiencing homelessness in the community and increasing access to supportive services. They developed clear metrics to measure progress towards these outcomes, such as the number of people housed, the length of time they remained housed, and their overall well-being.

The foundation gathered data and feedback from a range of stakeholders, including grantees, beneficiaries, and community members. They conducted a thorough analysis of the effectiveness of their grant programs and their impact on the community. They compared the results of their evaluations to industry standards and best practices to ensure that they were achieving the highest possible impact.

Based on their evaluations, the foundation made necessary adjustments to their programs and services to better serve their beneficiaries and communities. They created a culture of continuous learning and improvement by regularly assessing the impact of their foundation and sharing their findings with stakeholders, including donors, funders, and grantors.

As a result of their evaluation framework, the foundation was able to demonstrate their commitment to making a positive impact on homelessness in their community. They were able to track progress towards their desired outcomes and make adjustments as needed to ensure that their grants were having the maximum impact. Regularly sharing the results and findings with stakeholders allowed the foundation to boost confidence and support in its mission, resulting in significant funding growth and the attraction of new donors.

Eliminating Low-Value Programs

In the quest to optimize the effectiveness of a nonprofit organization that is in line with its mission, it is imperative to regularly evaluate the impact of its programs and services. The ultimate goal is to allocate resources in a way that best serves the needs of its beneficiaries and maximizes positive impact in the community.

To effectively eliminate low-value programs, an organization must first identify its objectives and goals. By understanding the purpose behind the programs and services being offered, the organization can determine which programs align with these objectives and which do not.

(Remember, everything should start and end with the organization's mission in mind.)

In this list, we will outline the key steps a nonprofit should take to identify and eliminate low-value programs, ensuring that its efforts are focused on areas where it can have the greatest impact. By streamlining its operations and removing inefficiencies, a nonprofit can better serve its mission and achieve its desired outcomes.

1. **Identify low-value programs:** The first step in eliminating low-value programs is to identify them. This can be done by analyzing program outcomes and feedback from stakeholders and comparing the program to similar initiatives.
2. **Assess the impact:** Once low-value programs have been identified, it is important to assess their impact. This involves analyzing the program's goals, outcomes, and resources used to determine its effectiveness and efficiency.

3. **Evaluate alternative options:** Before eliminating a low-value program, it is essential to evaluate alternative options. This can include enhancing the existing program, merging it with another initiative, or finding a more efficient solution.

4. **Communicate with stakeholders:** Before making any changes, it is important to communicate with stakeholders and explain why the program is being eliminated. This includes members, funders, staff, clients, and other partners.

5. **Reallocate resources:** The resources used in low-value programs should be reallocated to higher-impact initiatives. This includes funding, staff, and volunteers.

6. **Implement changes:** Once a plan for eliminating low-value programs has been developed, it is important to implement the changes. This can include modifying the program, ending it, or redirecting resources to other initiatives.

7. **Monitor progress:** Regular monitoring of progress and outcomes is crucial to ensure that the changes are having the desired effect.

8. **Evaluate impact:** After a specified period of time, it is important to evaluate the impact of the changes. This can be done by analyzing the program's goals, outcomes, and resources used to determine its effectiveness and efficiency.

9. **Engage stakeholders:** Regular engagement with stakeholders, including members, partners, funders, volunteers, and staff, can help ensure that changes are being made in a transparent and collaborative manner.

10. **Continuously improve:** The process of eliminating low-value programs is an ongoing one. Regular assessments and continuous improvement initiatives can help ensure that a nonprofit is delivering the most impactful and efficient programs possible.

Nonprofits can employ various approaches to identify and, in some cases, enhance low-value programs. These methods include:

- Conducting regular surveys and focus groups with members, stakeholders, and community members to gather feedback on program and service delivery.

- Performing cost-benefit analysis to determine the cost-effectiveness of programs and services and identify areas for improvement.
- Collaborating with other organizations to pool resources and share best practices.
- Using data and technology to track outcomes and measure progress.
- Regularly reviewing program and service outcomes and adjusting strategies as needed.
- Engaging in quality improvement initiatives to continuously refine and improve program and service delivery.
- Developing partnerships with other organizations and stakeholders to increase program and service impact.
- Implementing an internal evaluation process to regularly assess program and service performance and identify areas for improvement.

By using a combination of these strategies, nonprofits can ensure that their programs and services are delivering maximum impact and return on investment.

Common Mistakes

There are several common mistakes that nonprofit organizations can make when evaluating programs and services. Some of these mistakes include:

- **Lack of clear objectives and goals:** Without clear objectives and goals for programs, it can be difficult to accurately measure the success of them.

- **Insufficient data and information:** Gathering data and information is critical to evaluating programs and services, but organizations must make sure they are gathering the right data.

- **Ignoring feedback from stakeholders:** Stakeholder feedback can provide valuable insights into the strengths and weaknesses of programs and services. Ignoring this feedback can lead to missed opportunities for improvement.

- **Focusing on short-term goals instead of long-term outcomes:** While it is important to see quick results, it is also important to focus on the long-term outcomes that a program or service is designed to achieve.

- **Not comparing programs and services to best practices:** By benchmarking against best practices, organizations can learn from the experiences of others and identify areas for improvement.

- **Lack of resources and funding:** Improving programs and services requires adequate resources, including funding, staff, and volunteers. Without these resources, it can be difficult to put improvement plans into action.

- **Inadequate monitoring and evaluation:** Regular monitoring and evaluation is essential to track progress and make adjustments as needed. Without this, it can be difficult to know if a program or service is truly effective.

An example of how a nonprofit membership association's failure to conduct proper research before launching a new program led to its discontinuation can be seen in the case of a healthcare professionals' association.

A nonprofit membership association for healthcare professionals wanted to expand their offerings to provide online courses for their members. The association believed that this program would be well-received, as they had received positive feedback from a few members they had spoken with in the past.

Without conducting proper research or engaging with a larger group of members, the nonprofit went ahead and launched the online course. Unfortunately, the program did not achieve the expected success, and the organization struggled to gain traction.

As it turned out, many members were not interested in taking online courses, and preferred in-person workshops and seminars instead. Additionally, the nonprofit had not considered the time and cost required to develop and maintain an online course, and had underestimated the competition from other organizations offering similar services.

The program was eventually discontinued due to lack of interest and the financial burden it placed on the nonprofit. This experience taught the organization the importance of conducting proper research and engaging with a diverse group of members before launching new programs. By doing so, the organization would have been better equipped to make data-driven decisions about the viability of the program, the best delivery methods, and the time and cost required to develop and maintain it. This would have saved the association time and resources and avoided the disappointment of investing in a program that failed to achieve the desired results.

Ultimately, proper research and engagement are critical for nonprofit organizations seeking to make informed decisions and effectively deliver on their mission and goals.

When to Sunset Programs and Services

In the context of evaluating programs and services, the decision to sunset a program or service should not be taken lightly.

The importance of this decision lies in the understanding that resources, both time and funding, are limited. While it may be tempting to continue investing in a program or service that has been a part of the organization for a long time, it is crucial to evaluate its impact and effectiveness in achieving the organization's goals. It is only then that a well-informed decision can be made, either to sunset a program or service that is no longer aligned with the organization's objectives or to continue supporting it with necessary resources.

The goal of evaluating and improving programs and services is to maximize the impact and return on investment, ensuring that resources are being used effectively and efficiently to achieve the organization's mission.

Sunsetting a program or service is a significant decision for any nonprofit organization, as it often involves reallocating resources, letting go of staff, and potentially disappointing stakeholders or board members who helped develop the program. However, it can also be a valuable step in refining an organization's mission, focusing on areas where it can have the greatest impact, and streamlining operations.

Here are ten steps for a successful program or service sunsetting process:

1. **Define the objectives:** Clearly articulate the reasons for considering sunsetting the program or service. Does it provide a return on mission?

2. **Gather data and feedback:** Collect relevant data and feedback from stakeholders, including staff, clients, partners, and funders. Determine the impact and effort of every program, benefit, and service.

3. **Conduct a thorough analysis:** Analyze the program or service in light of its impact and effectiveness, including a comparison to best practices. This type of analysis will pay off in the long run and contribute to a data-driven decision-making process.

4. **Engage stakeholders:** Facilitate stakeholder engagement, including staff, members, volunteers, and other partners, to gather additional feedback and understanding. Find out why there is low utilization and if there is an opportunity to salvage it.

5. **Identify key issues:** Identify the key issues that are leading to the consideration of sunsetting the program or service.

6. **Develop a sunsetting plan:** Create a detailed plan for sunsetting the program or service,

including goals, strategies, and timelines. Remember, winding down a program may take some time.

7. **Allocate resources:** Consider the resources required to support the sunsetting plan, including funding, staff, and volunteers.

8. **Communicate the decision:** Communicate the decision to sunset the program or service transparently and proactively with all stakeholders. This should include detail on how the decision was made and how it relates back to the organization's mission.

9. **Reallocate resources:** Reallocate resources, including staff and funding, to support other programs or services. This is a great opportunity to boost staff efforts in successful programs.

10. **Continuously evaluate:** Continuously evaluate the impact of the sunsetted program or service, including any unintended consequences and lessons learned.

Evaluating and improving programs and services is a crucial aspect of any nonprofit organization's operations. By regularly assessing the impact and effectiveness of these initiatives, nonprofits can make informed decisions about how to allocate resources, optimize their strategies, and ultimately achieve their mission.

With a systematic approach and a focus on continuous improvement, nonprofits can ensure that they are delivering the best possible outcomes for the members and communities they serve. By avoiding common mistakes and being proactive about sunsetting programs that no longer align with the organization's goals, nonprofits can maximize their impact and remain relevant in today's rapidly changing world.

Chapter Ten: Understanding Legal and Risk

The typical legal structure of a nonprofit organization is a non-stock corporation or a trust.

Non-stock corporations are established under state law and must be registered with the secretary of state or similar office. They are also exempt from paying federal income taxes under Section 501(c) of the Internal Revenue Code.

Trusts are another common legal structure for nonprofits and are established by a grantor who transfers property to a trustee to hold and manage for the benefit of a specific purpose or group of beneficiaries (i.e., a charitable trust that is established to provide scholarships for underprivileged students).

Though non-stock corporations and trusts are the most common legal structures of nonprofit organizations, they may also adopt other legal structures, such as a cooperative or a limited liability company (LLC).

Cooperatives are organizations that are owned and governed by their members, who are typically the beneficiaries of the organization's services. In a cooperative structure, members have a say in the decision-making process and share in the profits or benefits of the organization. This structure can be a good fit for nonprofits that prioritize member empowerment and democracy, such as worker or housing cooperatives.

LLCs, on the other hand, are a hybrid form of business that combines the liability protection of a corporation with the tax benefits and flexibility of a partnership. For nonprofits, the key advantage of an LLC structure is the limited liability protection it offers, which can protect the personal assets of the organization's leaders and members from business debts and obligations. This can be especially appealing for nonprofits that operate in high-risk industries or that have significant financial obligations.

While cooperatives and LLCs can be a viable option for some nonprofits, it's important to understand the specific requirements and responsibilities that come with each structure, as well as any legal and tax implications. Before making a decision, it's recommended that nonprofits seek guidance from legal and financial experts and carefully consider their unique needs and goals.

Subsidiaries

In the world of nonprofits, it is important to understand the different organizational structures available to further the mission and goals of the organization. One such structure is a subsidiary—a separate legal entity that operates under the umbrella of a larger parent organization, usually a nonprofit.

For example, A 501(c)(6) business or trade association may choose to establish a 501(c)(3) organization to tap into the benefits that come with the 501(c)(3) status. The 501(c)(3) status grants a nonprofit tax-exempt status and allows it to receive tax-deductible contributions, which can significantly increase the pool of potential donors.

Additionally, the 501(c)(3) status may enhance the reputation and credibility of the organization and allow it to apply for grants and other funding opportunities that are only available to these types of tax-exempt organizations.

Furthermore, as mentioned in a previous chapter, the establishment of a 501(c)(3) subsidiary can provide the parent organization with a separate legal entity to conduct certain activities, while still maintaining the benefits of its 501(c)(6) status.

Let us examine the key advantages of establishing a subsidiary:

- **Flexibility:** A subsidiary allows nonprofits to quickly respond to new opportunities and changing circumstances.
- **Increased efficiency:** Subsidiaries can help streamline operations by allowing organizations to focus on specific projects or initiatives.
- **Financial stability:** By creating a subsidiary, nonprofits can insulate their main operations from financial risks associated with new programs and services.

- **Better risk management:** Subsidiaries provide a level of legal protection to the parent organization, separating liabilities and reducing the risk of losing assets.

- **Increased capacity:** A subsidiary can bring in new resources and expertise to help the parent organization achieve its goals.

- **Improved governance:** Subsidiaries can be governed separately, allowing for a clear separation of responsibilities between the parent organization and its subsidiary.

- **Increased funding opportunities:** Subsidiaries can access different sources of funding, including grants and donations, that may not be available to the parent organization.

- **Branding opportunities:** Subsidiaries can create a separate brand and marketing strategy, helping the parent organization reach new audiences.

- **Potential for revenue generation:** Subsidiaries can generate revenue to support the parent organization and its mission.

- **Expansion of services**: A subsidiary can provide a platform for the parent organization to expand its services and reach new beneficiaries.

Here is an example:

A nonprofit organization providing services for children with disabilities successfully established a subsidiary to expand its services and reach new beneficiaries. The parent organization identified a gap in the market for providing specialized therapy services to children with autism and other developmental disabilities, but did not have the resources or capacity to launch a new program within its existing operations.

The organization created a subsidiary to specifically focus on providing these services, while also insulating its main operations from the financial risks associated with launching a new program. The subsidiary was governed separately, with its own board of directors and staff, allowing for a clear separation of responsibilities and improved governance.

Through the subsidiary, the organization was able to access different sources of funding, including grants and donations, that were not available to the parent organization. The subsidiary also provided a platform to generate revenue to support the parent organization and its mission.

Additionally, the subsidiary brought in new resources and expertise, expanding the organization's capacity to provide services and increasing efficiency. The subsidiary also allowed for flexibility to quickly respond to new opportunities and changing circumstances in the market.

Overall, the establishment of the subsidiary allowed the nonprofit organization to expand its services, reach new beneficiaries, and generate revenue to support its mission, while also insulating its main operations from financial risks and improving governance.

In short, establishing a subsidiary can help a nonprofit to achieve its mission more effectively and efficiently, making it an important consideration for any nonprofit looking to grow and enhance its impact.

Governing Documents

As a nonprofit organization, it is crucial to have a comprehensive and well-defined set of governing documents that outline the purpose, values, and objectives of the organization. These documents serve as a blueprint for decision-making and operations, ensuring that all actions are aligned with the mission and goals of the nonprofit.

In this section, we will delve into the importance of six essential governing documents that are vital to the success of any nonprofit: the mission statement, articles of incorporation, bylaws, policies, the strategic plan, and the annual budget.

Each document has a unique role in guiding the nonprofit towards its desired outcomes and impact. By gaining a comprehensive understanding of each document and how they work together, a nonprofit can ensure that its operations run efficiently and effectively.

- **Mission statement (purpose for existence; IRS submission):** A mission statement is a concise, compelling, and inspirational declaration of the purpose, vision, and values of an organization. It outlines the organization's reason for existence, who it serves, and what it seeks to accomplish. The mission statement serves as a guiding principle for the nonprofit's decision-making and helps to focus its efforts and resources towards achieving its goals.

- **Articles of incorporation (relationship to state government):** The articles of incorporation, also known as the certificate of incorporation, is the legal document that establishes a nonprofit as a corporation in the eyes of the state. It outlines the basic information of the organization—such as its name, purpose, location, and structure—and lays the foundation for the nonprofit's governance and operations.

- **Bylaws (relationship between board and stakeholders):** Bylaws are the governing rules and procedures of a nonprofit organization. They outline the duties and responsibilities of the board of directors, the roles of staff, and the process for conducting meetings and elections. Bylaws also set forth the rules for amending the organization's governing documents and provide a framework for the nonprofit's governance and decision-making.

- **Policies (interpretation of bylaws, wisdom of prior boards):** Policies are written statements that outline the nonprofit's stance on a specific issue or subject. They provide guidance for the organization's operations, decision-making, and behavior, and ensure consistency and alignment with the organization's mission and values.

- **Strategic plan (roadmap for the organization):** A strategic plan is a comprehensive roadmap that outlines the nonprofit's goals, objectives, strategies, and actions for achieving its mission over a specified period of time. The plan helps the nonprofit to prioritize its efforts, allocate resources effectively, and measure its progress towards achieving its goals.

- **Annual budget (financial projection and position):** An annual budget is a financial plan that outlines the nonprofit's expected income and expenditures for a given fiscal year. It serves as a tool for managing the organization's finances and helps to ensure that the nonprofit has the resources it needs to achieve its goals and deliver its programs and services.

The budget also provides a basis for monitoring the organization's financial performance and making informed decisions about future expenditures and resource allocation. The budget plays a critical role in ensuring that sufficient resources are directed towards achieving the organization's strategic goals and objectives.

Policies

As a nonprofit organization, having a set of clear and comprehensive policies is crucial for ensuring effective operations and decision-making. These policies serve as the foundation for the organization's ethical standards and values, guiding the behavior of its staff, volunteers, and board members. Developing and maintaining these policies is essential for maintaining the organization's integrity, accountability, and transparency.

In this list, we will explore a range of policies that are essential for nonprofits to have in place. From financial management to human resources, each policy serves a unique purpose in supporting the organization's mission and goals.

By having these policies in place, nonprofits can ensure that they are operating in a responsible and ethical manner, while also promoting a positive and productive work environment. Whether you are a newly formed nonprofit or an established organization, this list provides a comprehensive guide to help ensure that your policies are in line with industry standards and best practices.

1. **Conflict of interest policy:** This outlines the ethical standards and procedures for addressing potential conflicts of interest within the organization.
2. **Whistleblower policy:** This outlines the process for reporting unethical or illegal

behavior within the organization and provides protection for those who make such reports.

3. **Financial management policy:** This outlines the financial management practices, including budgeting, accounting, and financial reporting, that the organization adheres to.

4. **Procurement policy:** This outlines the procedures and standards for purchasing goods and services for the organization.

5. **Human resources policy:** This outlines the policies and procedures the paid CEO uses for hiring, compensating, and managing staff within the organization.

6. **Privacy policy:** This outlines how the organization collects, stores, and uses personal information and data.

7. **Fundraising policy:** This outlines the procedures and standards for soliciting and accepting donations, grants, and other forms of support.

8. **Board governance policy:** This outlines the roles and responsibilities of the board of directors and the procedures for their meetings and decision-making processes.

9. **Volunteer management policy:** This outlines the recruitment, selection, and management of volunteers within the organization.

10. **Program evaluation policy:** This outlines the procedures for evaluating the effectiveness and impact of the organization's programs and services.

The question of the appropriate number of policies for a nonprofit organization to implement is a frequent topic of discussion. The common number of policies a nonprofit should have in place varies based on the size and complexity of the organization. A small organization may have just a few policies, while larger nonprofits may have dozens or even hundreds of policies covering various aspects of their operations.

However, the important thing is not the number of policies, but the thoroughness and effectiveness of the policies in guiding the organization towards its mission and goals. The policies should cover the critical areas of the organization, such as financial management, fundraising, human resources, and governance, among others.

Keeping policies up to date is crucial for maintaining the organization's legal compliance, ethical standards, and overall effectiveness. One approach to accomplishing this is to regularly review the policies, taking into account changes in laws, regulations, and best practices in the industry.

Another effective method is to establish a policy review committee, composed of board members, staff, and external experts, to oversee the process and provide recommendations for updates.

In addition, engaging with stakeholders, such as members, donors, beneficiaries, and community members, can provide valuable insight and help ensure that the policies align with the organization's mission and values. It's also important to have a clear and easily accessible process for policy updates, including clear communication and training for all staff and volunteers on the updated policies.

Risk Awareness and Avoidance

In today's rapidly changing world, risk is an inevitable aspect of any organization's operations. For nonprofits, it is especially important to understand and effectively manage risk, as the consequences of neglecting to do so can have a significant impact on their mission and ability to deliver services to their beneficiaries.

A lack of risk awareness and preparation can lead to negative outcomes such as financial loss, reputational damage, and failure to achieve important goals.

By taking proactive steps to identify and mitigate risks, nonprofits can ensure that they are able to operate effectively and fulfill their purpose with confidence. Familiarizing oneself with the various forms of risk and implementing appropriate strategies to avoid them is crucial for the long-term success, sustainability, and longevity of any organization.

The steps in managing risk can be divided into several stages:

1. **Identify risks:** The first step in managing risks for a nonprofit is to identify potential areas of vulnerability. This could include financial risks, operational risks, reputation risks, and more.

2. **Assess the risks:** Once potential risks have been identified, it is important to assess the likelihood and potential impact of each risk. This information can be used to prioritize risks and develop a plan for managing them.

3. **Develop a risk management plan:** Based on the assessment of risks, a nonprofit should develop a comprehensive risk management plan that includes strategies for avoiding, mitigating, or transferring risks. This plan should be reviewed and updated regularly.

4. **Implement risk management strategies:** The risk management plan should be put into action, with strategies being implemented to minimize the impact of identified risks.

5. **Monitor and review:** It is important to regularly monitor and review the effectiveness

of the risk management plan and strategies, making any necessary adjustments to ensure ongoing protection.

6. **Communicate and educate:** It is essential that all stakeholders, including board members, staff, volunteers, and stakeholders are aware of the risks faced by the organization and their role in managing them. Regular training and communication about risk management is important for building a culture of risk awareness.

Risk Management Plan

A comprehensive risk management plan for a nonprofit should have several key elements to effectively mitigate potential risks and ensure the organization's success. These elements include a risk assessment process, identification of critical assets and vulnerabilities, development of contingency plans, regular review and evaluation of the plan, and communication and training for all stakeholders.

Additionally, the plan should prioritize risk mitigation strategies, allocate resources appropriately, and have a designated person or team responsible for implementing and monitoring the plan. With these elements in place, an organization can proactively manage risks and ensure the achievement of its mission and goals.

A risk management plan for a nonprofit should include the following elements:

- **Risk assessment:** The process of identifying and evaluating potential risks to the organization and its operations.
- **Risk register:** A comprehensive and organized list of all identified risks, their likelihood, potential impact, and mitigation strategies.
- **Risk mitigation:** The steps taken to minimize the likelihood or impact of identified risks.
- **Risk monitoring:** The ongoing process of tracking and evaluating the effectiveness of risk mitigation strategies.
- **Crisis management plan:** A plan outlining the steps to be taken in the event of a crisis or unexpected event, such as a natural disaster, cyber-attack, or sudden loss of key personnel.

- **Insurance review:** A review of the organization's insurance coverage to ensure adequate protection against potential losses.
- **Staff training:** Providing staff with the knowledge and skills necessary to identify and address risks.
- **Regular review:** Periodic review and update of the risk management plan to ensure it remains relevant and effective.

These elements are critical components of a comprehensive risk management plan, designed to help a nonprofit minimize the impact of risks and ensure its long-term sustainability.

Apparent and Actual Authority

Board members are entrusted with a great deal of responsibility and power to make decisions on behalf of the organization. However, it's important to understand the distinction between apparent and actual authority and the potential consequences of overstepping these boundaries.

Apparent authority refers to the power that others perceive a board member to have, even if that power does not actually exist. Actual authority, on the other hand, is the power that a board member actually has, as defined by the organization's bylaws, mission, and governing documents.

It's crucial for board members to understand the distinction between these two types of authority and to ensure that their actions are within the bounds of their actual authority. Failure to do so can lead to disastrous consequences for both the organization and the individual board member.

Consider a situation where a board member, acting on what they believed was their apparent authority, made a major financial decision without consulting the rest of the board or following the organization's established procedures. As a result of this decision, the organization suffered significant financial losses and was forced to lay off staff and cut programs.

In this scenario, the board member had overstepped their actual authority and had acted in a way that was detrimental to the organization. As a result, the board member may face legal action or be held personally liable for the financial losses incurred by the organization.

It's important to note that directors and officers, as well as other protections, may not apply to the board member in this scenario. It's ultimately the responsibility of the board member to ensure that their actions are within the bounds of their actual authority and in the best interests of the organization. That is why board training and development is so critical.

In conclusion, understanding the distinction between apparent and actual authority is essential for board members. Failure to do so can have serious consequences for the organization and the individual board member. Board members must ensure that their actions are within the bounds of their actual authority and in compliance with the organization's bylaws, mission, and governing documents.

Protections for the Board

Running a nonprofit organization comes with its own set of challenges, including legal and financial responsibilities that board members must navigate.

As a nonprofit board member, it is important to understand the various protections available to you, both at the state and federal level, that can help shield you from personal liability in the event of legal disputes. They are as follows:

- **Business judgment rule**: The business judgment rule assumes that board members have acted in good faith and in the best interests of the organization unless there is evidence to the contrary. Board members are generally not held personally liable for decisions made on behalf of the organization unless they have engaged in gross negligence, willful misconduct, or a breach of their fiduciary duties.
- **Directors and officers (D&O) liability insurance**: Nonprofit board members are often protected by D&O liability insurance, which covers the costs of legal defense and damages arising from lawsuits against board members for actions taken in their official capacity.
- **Indemnification**: Nonprofit organizations may provide indemnification to board members, which reimburses them for legal costs and

damages incurred in connection with their service on the board.

- **Duty of care**: Board members have a duty of care to the organization, which requires them to act with care, diligence, and in the best interests of the organization. To fulfill this duty, board members should be informed and engaged in the organization's activities, participate in decision-making, and avoid conflicts of interest.

- **Duty of loyalty**: Board members have a duty of loyalty to the organization, which requires them to act in the best interests of the organization, rather than their personal interests. To fulfill this duty, board members should avoid conflicts of interest, disclose any potential conflicts, and recuse themselves from decision-making when appropriate.

- **State and federal protections**: Nonprofit board members may be protected by state and federal laws that regulate the formation and operation of nonprofit organizations, as well as volunteer immunity acts at both the state and federal level. For example, the Federal Volunteer Protection Act and many state laws provide protection for volunteers serving nonprofit organizations from liability for harm caused by their actions, as long as the harm was not intentional or the result of gross negligence.

- **Limited liability corporation (LLC) protection**: If the nonprofit organization is structured as an LLC, board members may be protected by limited liability, meaning that their personal assets are generally not at risk in the event of a lawsuit against the organization. However, it is important to note that in some cases, the LLC corporate veil may be pierced, meaning that board members may be held personally liable for the actions of the organization. This may occur if the organization engages in illegal or fraudulent activities, if the organization is not properly maintained, or if the board members commingle personal and organizational assets. Therefore, while an LLC structure can provide some protection for board members, it is crucial to ensure that the organization is properly managed and operates within the law to avoid personal liability.

Importance of Antitrust Awareness and Avoidance

Antitrust laws prohibit anti-competitive behavior and promote fair competition in the market. It is important for nonprofit board members to be aware of antitrust laws and avoid any actions that could result in antitrust violations. Antitrust violations can occur on a board of directors through various actions, including:

- Discussing pricing strategies or other sensitive competitive information with competitors or industry peers, which could be interpreted as collusion.
- Sharing confidential information about business operations or customers with competitors, which could lead to market allocation or bid-rigging.
- Excluding or boycotting competitors or suppliers, which could result in anticompetitive behavior.
- Attempting to monopolize the market by engaging in unfair practices that limit competition and prevent new entrants from entering the market.

To avoid antitrust violations, nonprofit organizations should take the following steps:

- Develop an antitrust policy and include it in the organization's bylaws.
- Distribute the policy to all board members, staff, and volunteers, and review it at every meeting.
- Provide antitrust training for board members, staff, and volunteers on a regular basis.
- Monitor activities to ensure compliance with antitrust laws, including monitoring meetings, discussions, and interactions with competitors.
- Avoid discussing or exchanging sensitive information with competitors, such as pricing, discounts, or customer data.
- Consider working with legal counsel to review activities that may have antitrust implications, such as joint ventures or mergers.
- Establish an antitrust compliance program, including an antitrust compliance officer, to oversee and enforce compliance with antitrust laws.

- Keep accurate records of all meetings and discussions with competitors, including agendas and meeting minutes.
- Have an antitrust sign-in sheet at each meeting, where attendees acknowledge the antitrust policy and certify that they understand and will comply with it.

Antitrust violations can result in significant fines and penalties for nonprofit organizations. Under federal law, violations of antitrust laws can result in fines of up to $100 million for corporations, or up to $1 million and 10 years in prison for individuals.

In addition to federal penalties, states may also have their own antitrust laws and penalties that organizations must comply with. Antitrust violations can also result in civil lawsuits from competitors, customers, or other affected parties, which can result in damages, injunctive relief, and attorney's fees. Finally, antitrust violations can result in significant reputational harm for nonprofit organizations, potentially impacting their ability to attract members, donors, and supporters.

Chapter Eleven: Leveraging Technology

In this fast-paced digital world, technology plays a significant role in the operations of modern organizations, including nonprofits. Adopting the right technology solutions can help nonprofits achieve their mission more effectively, streamline their processes, and increase their impact. As such, it is critical to understand how they can leverage technology to achieve their goals and stay ahead of the curve.

In this section, we will explore the various ways that nonprofits can effectively use technology to enhance their operations and achieve their mission. From utilizing cloud computing, to taking advantage of social media, to using data analytics, we will provide a comprehensive guide on how to make the most out of technology and achieve success in today's digital age.

Introduction to the Use of Technology in the Nonprofit Sector

In the nonprofit sector, technology plays a critical role in helping organizations achieve their mission and reach their goals. With the rise of digital tools and platforms, nonprofits are now able to operate more efficiently and effectively, engage with stakeholders more authentically, and reach new audiences with their message. Nonprofits use technology in a variety of ways, including:

- **Communication and collaboration:** Technology can be utilized to communicate and collaborate with stakeholders, including members, donors, volunteers, staff, board members, and partners. They can use email, instant messaging, videoconferencing, and project management tools to streamline communication and increase collaboration.
- **Fundraising:** Technology is playing an ever increasingly important role in the fundraising process. Many organizations use online fundraising platforms to accept donations,

manage campaigns, and build fundraising pages.

- **Data management:** Nonprofits collect and store large amounts of data, including membership and financial records, donor information, volunteer data, and program outcomes. Technology can help manage this data in a secure and efficient manner, providing insights and facilitating data-driven decision-making.

- **Program delivery:** Nonprofits can use technology to deliver their programs and services more effectively, reaching larger audiences and providing more impact. For example, organizations can use online platforms to provide education, training, and support to their members and constituents.

- **Advocacy:** Nonprofits can leverage technology to advocate for their cause and raise awareness about their mission. They can use social media, websites, and digital campaigns to reach a wider audience and engage with their stakeholders.

Overall, technology has revolutionized the way nonprofits operate, providing them with the tools and platforms they need to achieve their mission and drive positive impact in their communities. This technology is moving at such a fast pace that it may be difficult to keep up with all of the changes.

Benefits of Technology for Nonprofits

Technology has become an indispensable tool in today's digital age and the benefits are many. By leveraging technology, nonprofits can streamline their operations, increase efficiency, and engage with their stakeholders more effectively.

Here are some key benefits that technology can bring to nonprofits:

- **Increased efficiency:** Technology can automate manual tasks and reduce the administrative burden on staff. This can free up time and resources that can be redirected to mission-critical activities.
- **Better engagement:** Technology can provide new and innovative ways to engage with

stakeholders, including members, donors, volunteers, and constituents. For example, social media platforms, email marketing, and text messaging can help nonprofits reach a wider audience, build stronger member relationships, and drive fundraising efforts.

- **Improved data management:** Technology can help nonprofits collect, manage, and analyze data more effectively, enabling them to make data-driven decisions that can improve their impact.

- **Greater accessibility:** By using technology, nonprofits can provide their services and information to a wider audience, including individuals who may not have access to traditional channels.

Adopting technology can bring numerous benefits to nonprofits, particularly foundations and membership associations. These organizations have a crucial role in driving change and making an impact in their industries, professions, and communities, and technology can help them achieve these goals more efficiently and effectively. By embracing technology, they can streamline their operations, increase engagement with members and stakeholders, and reach a wider audience.

The consequences of being left behind in terms of technology adoption can be severe. Organizations that do not embrace technology may find it more difficult to compete for funding and support, as donors and members increasingly expect organizations to use technology to operate more efficiently and effectively.

Additionally, organizations that are slow to adopt technology may find it difficult to attract and retain staff and volunteers, who are often familiar with and expect to use technology in their work.

Finally, organizations that do not embrace technology may miss out on opportunities to engage with their supporters and reach new audiences, which could limit their impact and ability to achieve their mission.

Commonly Used Technology

In the nonprofit sector, technology has become a powerful tool to help organizations achieve their missions more efficiently and effectively.

A number of different types of technology have been developed specifically, including nonprofit membership management software, donor management software, cloud computing, and social media platforms. These technologies can be leveraged in a number of different ways to help organizations meet their goals, improve their operations, and connect with their stakeholders more effectively.

Nonprofit membership management software refers to a suite of digital tools and platforms that help nonprofit organizations manage and track their membership base. These tools allow the storing and organization of critical data—such as contact information, membership status, and payment history—in a centralized database. With this information readily available, nonprofits can better understand their membership base, communicate more effectively with members, and streamline administrative processes.

Some of the key features of this software include membership sign-up and renewal, event and fundraising management, email communication and marketing, and reporting and data analytics. By utilizing these tools, organizations can increase efficiency, improve member engagement, and better allocate resources towards achieving their mission.

Membership management software can provide a range of benefits for organizations looking to streamline their processes and provide better engage opportunities. Some of the benefits are:

- **Automated member management:** Membership software can streamline the management of member information, including contact details, payment information, and member history.
- **Improved communication:** Built-in tools for email and newsletter management allow organizations to stay connected and engaged with members.

- **Enhanced member experiences:** Personalized dashboards and member portals provide a more engaging and satisfying membership experience.
- **Increased retention:** Offering members a range of benefits and resources can improve member satisfaction and reduce turnover.
- **Streamlined processes:** Automated membership renewals, payments, and other processes save time and increase efficiency.

As it relates to foundations and charities, donor management technology provides a comprehensive solution for effective management and communication. This type of software streamlines the process of tracking donor information, donations, and fundraising campaigns. With its advanced reporting capabilities, organizations are able to gain valuable insights into their base, monitor their fundraising performance, and make informed decisions for their future fundraising efforts.

The benefits include the following:

- **Contact management:** Donor management software often includes a contact database that stores information on all donors, including contact information, donation history, and demographic data. This feature makes it easy for nonprofits to manage their donor relationships and keep track of all interactions with donors.
- **Donation tracking:** This feature allows the tracking of all donations received, including the amount, date, and method of payment. This information can be used to generate reports, analyze donor behavior, and track the success of fundraising campaigns.
- **Fundraising campaigns:** Many donor management software platforms include tools to help create, manage, and track fundraising campaigns. This can include tools for creating donation pages, sending email appeals, and tracking the progress of each campaign.
- **Reporting capabilities:** A key benefit of donor management software is the ability to generate detailed reports on donations and donor

behavior. These reports can be used to analyze the effectiveness of fundraising campaigns, track trends in giving, and identify areas for improvement.

- **Communication tools:** Many donor management software platforms include tools for communicating with donors, including email, direct mail, and social media. These tools make it easier to reach out to donors, build relationships, and keep them engaged with their work.

- **Integration with other tools:** Some donor management software platforms can be integrated with other tools commonly used such as accounting software, payment processors, and customer relationship management (CRM) systems. This can help streamline operations and reduce the time spent on manual tasks.

Cloud computing is another type of technology that is being increasingly utilized among nonprofits. The following are the benefits of cloud computing:

- **Accessibility:** Cloud computing allows access to data from anywhere and at any time, which can be especially useful for organizations with staff working remotely or in different locations.
- **Cost savings:** By storing data in the cloud, organizations can save money on IT infrastructure and staffing costs.
- **Scalability:** The cloud can easily scale to meet changing needs by providing the necessary resources to handle growth and fluctuations in demand.
- **Improved collaboration:** Cloud computing provides the ability to collaborate and share information more easily, both within the organization and with partners and stakeholders.
- **Increased data security:** Storing data in the cloud is often more secure than storing it on-premise, as cloud providers have robust security measures in place to protect client data.

- **Improved data management:** Cloud computing provides more sophisticated data management tools—such as data backup, recovery, and analytics—that can help them make more informed decisions.

- **Enhanced mobile access:** By utilizing cloud technology, access to data and systems from mobile devices is enabled, allowing staff to be more productive while on the go.

- **Automated upgrades:** With cloud computing, organizations no longer have to worry about software upgrades or updates as these are handled automatically by the cloud provider.

Social media platforms like Facebook, Twitter, and Instagram are also commonly used by nonprofits to connect with their stakeholders, promote their missions, share news and updates, engage with followers, and even launch fundraising campaigns.

The following are some key benefits of utilizing social media platforms for nonprofits:

- **Reach a wider audience:** Social media platforms provide a cost-effective way to reach a large and diverse audience.
- **Build relationships:** By engaging with followers on social media, organizations can build more meaningful relationships with their stakeholders.
- **Share news and updates:** Organizations can use social media platforms to share news, updates, and other important information about their mission and work.
- **Launch fundraising and membership campaigns:** Social media platforms offer a variety of tools that can be used to launch fundraising campaigns, reach new donors and members, and track campaign progress.
- **Increase awareness:** By leveraging the power of social media, organizations can increase awareness of their cause and help drive more support for their mission.
- **Utilize automation:** Many social media platforms provide scheduling options and the

capability to identify content of interest and share it automatically with targeted audiences.

- **Access to analytics:** Most social media platforms provide access to powerful analytics tools that can help nonprofits measure the impact of their social media efforts and optimize their strategies over time.

Nonprofits can reap many benefits from embracing technology, including increased efficiency, improved engagement, and greater impact. By leveraging these tools, organizations can better achieve their missions and make a positive difference in the world.

Strategies for Selecting and Implementing Technology Solutions

Selecting and implementing the right technology solutions can be a challenging task. With the vast array of options available, it can be difficult to determine which solutions will best meet the needs of the organization. However, taking the time to carefully evaluate and select the right technology can help to streamline operations, improve communication and engagement with stakeholders, and increase overall efficiency and effectiveness.

In order to successfully select and implement technology solutions, it is important to have a clear understanding of goals, needs, and capabilities. Here are some effective strategies that could be considered:

- **Determine organizational needs and goals:** Before selecting a technology solution, it's essential to understand the specific needs and goals of the organization. This will help ensure that the solution selected is tailored to meet its unique needs.
- **Assess available options:** Research and evaluate different technology solutions available in the market. This includes evaluating the features and capabilities of each option, as well as their pricing and customer support.
- **Consider compatibility and integration:** When selecting a technology solution, it's essential to consider how well it integrates with existing systems and processes within the organization. This will help ensure a seamless

transition and minimize disruption to daily operations.

- **Consider scalability and future needs:** As the organization grows and evolves, it's essential to select a technology solution that can scale to meet future needs. This will help ensure the organization is well-positioned for long-term success.

- **Engage stakeholders:** Involve key stakeholders—including staff, board members, and others—in the selection and implementation process. This will help ensure that the solution selected is well-received and that the transition is smooth.

- **Develop a plan:** Once a solution has been selected, it's essential to develop a detailed plan for implementation. This should include a timeline, budget, and clear expectations for how the solution will be integrated into daily operations.

- **Provide training and support:** To ensure the success of the technology solution, it's essential to provide adequate training and support to staff and stakeholders. This will help ensure that the solution is used effectively and that everyone is confident in its use.

In conclusion, implementing technology solutions can greatly enhance the effectiveness of a nonprofit organization. However, it's essential to approach the selection and implementation process with great care, taking into consideration the specific needs and goals of the organization, as well as the available resources.

Also, don't skimp on the dollars that will be necessary to implement an effective and well-rounded approach. This is not the area to cut resources, given how much of the organization's decisions are data-driven.

By following a strategic and well-thought-out plan, nonprofits can ensure that their technology investments lead to long-term success and bring about significant benefits for their mission. Ultimately, by leveraging technology, they can better serve their stakeholders, achieve their goals, and make a greater impact in their communities.

Challenges and Risks of Technology Adoption

Technology adoption can be a complex and risky undertaking for any organization. Despite the many benefits of technology, organizations must be aware of the challenges and risks that come with implementing new technology solutions, particularly relating to security and data privacy.

Security

- **Cyber-attacks and hacking:** Nonprofits store sensitive information, such as donor information and financial data, making them an attractive target for cyber criminals. They must ensure that their technology solutions have robust security measures in place to protect against cyber-attacks and hacking.
- **Loss of data**: Technology can be vulnerable to failures or malfunctions, which can lead to the loss of critical data. Backup and disaster recovery plans need to be in place to mitigate the risk of data loss.
- **Physical theft**: Portable technology devices, such as laptops and smartphones, are

commonly used in nonprofits and are at risk of theft. Organizations must have strong physical security measures in place to protect their technology devices and data.

Data Privacy

- **Data breaches:** Data breaches can have severe consequences, including loss of reputation, donor trust, and legal liability. Organizations must ensure that their technology solutions have robust privacy and security measures in place to prevent data breaches.
- **Compliance:** Nonprofits must comply with a variety of data privacy laws and regulations, such as the General Data Protection Regulation (GDPR) and the Health Insurance Portability and Accountability Act (HIPAA). They must ensure that their technology solutions are compliant with these laws and regulations to avoid legal liability.
- **Donor trust:** Nonprofit foundations rely on donor trust to achieve their missions. Data breaches or failures to comply with data privacy laws can erode donor trust, which can

be difficult to regain. Nonprofits must ensure that their technology solutions respect the privacy and protect the data of their donors.

Cyber-Breach Insurance

Having cyber security insurance is important, because it protects organizations against the financial losses that can result from a cyber-attack or data breach.

With the increasing use of technology in the nonprofit sector, it is crucial for organizations to be prepared for the potential consequences of a cyber security incident. Nonprofits hold sensitive information about their members, donors, volunteers, clients, and operations, which, if compromised, could result in serious damage to the organization's reputation, loss of member and donor trust, and financial penalties.

Cyber security insurance is a type of insurance coverage that protects organizations against financial losses related to cyber-attacks, data breaches, and other technology-related risks.

This provides a safety net by covering the costs of responding to and recovering from a cyber-attack. These costs include legal expenses, crisis management costs (i.e. public relations efforts to repair an organization's reputation), notification costs, and expenses incurred to restore or recreate the affected systems and data. This insurance can help minimize the impact of a cyber security incident on a nonprofit's operations and mission.

Some of the common examples of cyber security insurance include:

- **First-party coverage:** Covers losses related to business interruption, cyber extortion, and system damage.
- **Third-party coverage:** Covers losses related to legal liability and damages owed to third parties as a result of a data breach or cyber-attack.
- **Privacy liability coverage:** Covers costs related to legal liability and damages owed to third parties for unauthorized access, disclosure, or misuse of personal information.

- **Network security liability coverage:** Covers losses related to legal liability and damages owed to third parties as a result of network security failure or failure to properly secure sensitive information.

- **Technology errors and omissions insurance:** Covers costs related to legal liability and damages owed to third parties as a result of technology-related errors or omissions.

It is important to have cyber security insurance because technology is increasingly being used in all aspects of nonprofit organizations, and the consequences of a data breach or cyber-attack can be severe and long-lasting. By having cyber security insurance, organizations can mitigate the financial risks associated with technology adoption and ensure that they are better prepared to respond to a technology-related crisis.

Given the rise in cyber-attacks, some insurers have now excluded cyber security insurance from its policies. It is important to contact your insurance company to determine your levels of coverage and if you need a rider to cover this cyber risk if it is not already included.

In conclusion, while technology offers many benefits, it is important to carefully consider the challenges and risks that come with technology adoption. Nonprofits must ensure that their technology solutions are secure, compliant, and respectful of member and donor privacy to achieve their missions.

Best Practices for Technology Management and Integration

Technology plays a crucial role in today's nonprofit sector, enabling organizations to achieve their missions more efficiently and effectively. However, the adoption of new technologies also comes with its own set of challenges and risks.

To ensure a smooth and successful technology integration, it is essential to have a comprehensive technology management strategy in place. In this section, we will explore the best practices for technology management and integration into an overall organizational strategy.

The following are best practices for technology integration:

- Develop a clear technology vision and strategy.
- Foster a culture of technology adoption and innovation.
- Assess technology needs regularly and proactively.
- Prioritize data security and privacy.
- Choose technology solutions that align with the organization's mission and goals.
- Invest in robust training and support for staff.
- Foster collaboration and communication between technology and non-technology teams.
- Ensure technology is accessible and inclusive for all stakeholders.
- Monitor and evaluate technology performance and impact regularly.
- Continuously assess and adjust technology strategy to keep pace with evolving organizational needs and advancements in technology.

By following these practices, nonprofits can ensure they are making the most of the opportunities that technology provides, while minimizing potential risks and challenges.

Elements of a Technology Management Plan

A comprehensive technology management plan is an important starting point and should address the following key points:

- **The organization's goals and objectives:** Clearly define the organization's technology goals and objectives and align them with the overall strategic plan.
- **An assessment of the current technology infrastructure:** Evaluate the organization's current technology infrastructure, including hardware, software, and networking systems.
- **Future technology needs:** Determine the organization's future technology needs based on its goals, objectives, and operational requirements.
- **Budget and funding sources:** Develop a budget that includes the cost of new

technology systems and ongoing maintenance and support.

- **Data security and privacy:** Develop policies and procedures to ensure the security and privacy of sensitive data and information.

- **Vendor and service provider management:** Choose and manage technology vendors and service providers that best meet the organization's needs.

- **Technical training and support:** Plan for and provide technical training and support for staff, volunteers, and other key stakeholders.

- **Technology integration:** Ensure that new technology systems integrate seamlessly with existing systems and processes.

- **Ongoing technology management:** Establish ongoing technology management processes, including regular technology assessments, upgrades, and maintenance.

- **Communication and collaboration:** Encourage communication and collaboration among staff, volunteers, and stakeholders to ensure successful technology adoption and integration.

Implementing technology within a nonprofit organization is a crucial step in ensuring its success and achieving its goals. While there may be some challenges and risks, these can be mitigated through careful planning, implementation, and management.

Large nonprofit organizations often have greater technology resources at their disposal, whether through an in-house team or consultants. Conversely, small nonprofit organizations may lack these resources and often rely on consultants to manage their technology needs. Regardless of the organization's size or the presence of an in-house team, adherence to best practices in technology management is essential. This will enable the organization to effectively utilize technology to meet its goals and objectives.

By following best practices, nonprofit organizations can maximize the potential of technology to drive efficiency, enhance donor and member engagement, and have a greater impact on their communities. A well-integrated technology strategy enables an organization to achieve its goals, expand its reach, and make a meaningful difference in the world.

Future Trends and Advancements in Technology

As technology continues to advance and evolve, it's important for nonprofits to stay informed and prepared for the latest developments and advancements. The nonprofit sector is often at the forefront of innovation and can greatly benefit from the latest technological advancements.

By keeping up with emerging trends, organizations can streamline their operations, engage with their stakeholders, and increase their impact.

The following is a list of the top 20 trends and advancements in technology for the nonprofit sector:

- **Artificial intelligence (AI) and machine learning (ML):** AI and ML will become more common in the nonprofit sector as organizations look for ways to automate processes and make more informed decisions.
- **Cloud computing:** Cloud computing will continue to grow in popularity as organizations look for cost-effective ways to store and access their data.

- **Big data analytics:** Nonprofits will use big data analytics to gain insights into their operations and make more informed decisions.

- **Mobile technology:** Mobile technology will play an ever increasingly important role as organizations look for ways to reach new audiences and engage with their stakeholders.

- **Internet of things (IoT):** IoT devices will allow organizations to collect and analyze data from various sources.

- **Virtual and augmented reality:** Virtual and augmented reality will become more common, providing organizations with new and innovative ways to engage with their stakeholders.

- **Cybersecurity:** Cybersecurity will remain a major concern, as organizations look for ways to protect their data and systems from cyber threats.

- **Blockchain technology:** Blockchain technology provides secure and transparent ways to manage data and transactions.

- **Social media platforms:** Social media platforms will allow organizations to connect with their stakeholders and promote their missions.

- **Digital fundraising:** Digital fundraising will reach new audiences and increase donations.

- **Chatbots:** Chatbots will become more common, establishing a new and innovative way to communicate with members, donors, and other stakeholders in a natural way.

- **Donor management software:** Donor management software will continue to play an important role as organizations look for ways to manage their donor data and improve donor engagement.

- **Video streaming:** Video streaming provides organizations with new and innovative ways to share their stories and reach new audiences.

- **Robotic process automation (RPA):** RPA will automate processes and improve efficiency.

- **Geolocation technology:** Geolocation technology will play an important role in targeting specific geographic areas to reach new audiences.

- **Collaborative tools:** Collaborative tools will provide organizations with new ways to collaborate and work together.

- **Cyber threat intelligence:** Cyber threat intelligence will allow organizations look for ways to protect their data and systems from cyber-attacks.

- **Social listening tools:** Social listening tools will allow organizations to monitor and respond to social media conversations about their brand.

- **Virtual conferencing:** Virtual conferencing will continue to expand and provide even more new ways for nonprofits to connect and engage with their stakeholders.

- **Digital transformation:** Digital transformation will continue to be a major trend as organizations look for ways to adopt new technologies and improve their operations.

Chapter Twelve: Communicating Your Story and Brand

Effective communication plays a critical role in the success of nonprofit organizations. It serves to establish a brand, build relationships with stakeholders, and disseminate the message effectively.

As we have touched on already, the advancement of technology has revolutionized the way nonprofits communicate, providing them with new and innovative platforms that allow for reaching a wider audience, engaging with stakeholders, and presenting their stories in a unique and captivating manner.

In this section, the various aspects of communicating a nonprofit's story and brand through technology will be explored, beginning with the development of a messaging strategy and the use of data to assess the impact of communication efforts.

Whether the goal is to create impactful social media campaigns, establish an online presence, or deepen connections with members, donors, and other stakeholders, this chapter will supply the necessary tools and insights to achieve success in story and brand communication.

Storytelling Through Social Media

Social media provides a unique platform for nonprofits to share their stories and connect with their audience in a powerful way. By utilizing engaging visuals, inspiring narratives, and interactive features, organizations can bring their mission and impact to life, inspiring followers to take action and support their cause. Whether through eye-catching graphics, heart-wrenching videos, or thought-provoking social media posts, the potential for engagement and mobilization of the audience is limitless.

The key to successful storytelling on social media lies in understanding the audience, crafting a compelling narrative, and using the appropriate tools and techniques to bring the story to life.

With the right strategy and execution, organizations can harness the power of social media to establish a strong brand, foster a sense of community, and ultimately maximize their impact.

Here are the top strategies and methods for effectively utilizing social media in sharing the story of your organization:

- **Audience identification:** Understanding the target audience will assist in tailoring the storytelling approach to their interests and preferences. Know them well and build the story for them.
- **Brand definition:** Developing a clear brand identity and message is crucial for effective storytelling on social media.
- **Content planning:** Planning ahead and implementing a content calendar ensures consistent flow of engaging and relevant content on social media.
- **Visual content creation:** Visual content, such as images and videos, is more effective in capturing attention and eliciting emotions compared to text alone.

- **Storytelling:** Utilize social media to share the organization's story, inspire with stories of those served, and demonstrate the impact of the work.

- **Audience engagement:** Encourage engagement with followers through asking questions, responding to comments, and fostering feedback.

- **Hashtag utilization:** Hashtags help categorize and increase the visibility of content to a wider audience.

- **Platform cross-promotion:** Utilizing multiple social media channels expands reach and enhances storytelling impact.

- **Measurement and adaptation:** Regularly assess the nonprofit's social media presence and adjust the strategy accordingly.

- **Trend and advancement awareness:** Stay current with the latest social media trends and advancements, and continuously seek new ways to improve storytelling efforts.

When considering the telling of a nonprofit's story, it is important to assess whether there are frequent statements by board members such as, "Our outreach is limited to the same ten people, and no one else knows about us." Effective utilization of social media for storytelling can assist nonprofits in expanding their reach to a broader audience, fostering stronger connections with stakeholders, and promoting their mission and brand.

By understanding and utilizing the different platforms and tools available, organizations can create compelling and impactful narratives that engage and inspire their followers. With careful planning and strategy, social media can be a powerful tool in the nonprofit's toolkit, helping to drive meaningful change and achieve their goals.

Evaluating Your Nonprofit's Digital Footprint

As a nonprofit organization, regularly assessing and evaluating the online presence through the website is crucial. The website serves as the initial point of contact with potential members, supporters, volunteers, donors, and other stakeholders, and is essential that it accurately reflects the organization and its mission.

Performing a thorough review of the website can help identify areas for improvement and facilitate the implementation of necessary changes to enhance its effectiveness and drive desired outcomes.

The following steps can assist in reviewing the current website and elevating its effectiveness:

- Evaluate the design and layout of the website for user-friendliness and aesthetic appeal.
- Analyze website content for relevance, timeliness, and effectiveness in communicating mission and goals.
- Check website functionality for ease of navigation and availability of necessary information for stakeholders.
- Assess search engine optimization (SEO) for use of relevant keywords and implementation of meta tags and descriptions.
- Consider the mobile experience for responsiveness and optimization for viewing on mobile devices.
- Evaluate user engagement for the duration of website visits, including interaction with different types of content.

- Assess integration with other marketing and communication channels for alignment with overall marketing strategy.
- Determine the conversion rate for visitors taking desired actions.
- Analyze website analytics for tracking of key metrics such as visitors, bounce rates, and conversion rates.
- Create a plan for improvement based on evaluation, identifying changes to enhance the website and effectively communicate the mission and goals.

Evaluating and refining the online presence of a nonprofit organization is essential for increasing impact. By considering key factors such as user experience, content strategy, and search engine optimization, organizations can make improvements to their online presence and attract new supporters while better serving existing ones.

To stay ahead of the curve, nonprofits must be proactive in optimizing their websites as technology continues to advance. An outdated and static website can be transformed into a dynamic platform that attracts members, donors, and other stakeholders with the latest information and trends. By adhering to best practices and creating a well-designed website, nonprofits can effectively communicate their story, engage with stakeholders, and make a greater impact. A dynamic and user-friendly website can also help to establish credibility and trust with stakeholders, leading to increased engagement and support for the organization's mission.

Crafting a Powerful Brand Message

Crafting a powerful brand message for an organization involves more than simply creating a tagline or mission statement; it involves discovering the underlying reason for the organization's work and communicating it in a manner that motivates others to support the mission.

As we discussed earlier, adopt Simon Sinek's philosophy, "People don't buy what you do, they buy why you do it."

It is crucial to understand the deeper purpose of the organization, and communicating it authentically and inspiringly can distinguish the organization from others and unite supporters around a shared cause or vision.

The days of merely having a "membership" are long gone. Communicating and developing a rallying cry around the organization's cause is what will inspire and attract members and stakeholders.

Developing a powerful brand message for a nonprofit is crucial for establishing a strong, recognizable, and impactful brand. Consider the following when creating the brand message:

- **Articulate the vision, mission, and values:** Clearly communicate the purpose, objectives, and beliefs of the organization, and distinguish it from others in the field.
- **Understand the audience:** Recognize the needs and motivations of the target audience and provide what they seek from the organization.
- **Maintain authenticity:** Stay true to the personality and values of the brand, and refrain from presenting a false image.

- **Formulate a straightforward message:** Make the message simple, memorable, and consistent across all communication channels.

- **Utilize emotional appeals:** Connect with the target audience by appealing to their emotions and emphasizing the cause the organization is impacting.

- **Evaluate and refine:** Continuously evaluate and refine the brand message to maintain its relevance to the target audience.

- **Align with actions:** Ensure that the brand message is reflected in all aspects of the organization, including its programs, services, and interactions with stakeholders.

Adherence to these guidelines allows for the crafting of a compelling brand message that effectively conveys the significance of a nonprofit and inspires action, support, and connection to its mission by its members, donors, and other key stakeholders. A robust brand message differentiates an organization, establishes trust and credibility, and ultimately drives positive impact and change.

One real-world example of a nonprofit that has built a powerful and engaging brand in its space is the Susan G. Komen Breast Cancer Foundation. The foundation has become synonymous with breast cancer awareness and research, and its signature pink ribbon has become a globally recognized symbol of the fight against breast cancer.

The foundation has successfully built its brand through a number of initiatives, including its annual Race for the Cure events, partnerships with major corporations, and extensive social media and online campaigns. The foundation has also been highly successful in engaging with its supporters, including breast cancer survivors and their families, through personal stories and testimonials that highlight the impact of the organization's work.

By building a strong and recognizable brand, the Susan G. Komen Foundation has been able to effectively communicate its message and engage a large and dedicated community of supporters. This has enabled the organization to raise significant funds for breast cancer research and awareness, and make a real impact in the fight against this devastating disease.

Creating Visually Engaging Content

By adhering to a strategic approach, nonprofits can turn dull content into visually captivating content. Visual communication has become a critical aspect of modern communication and has proven to boost engagement, drive conversions, and foster stronger relationships with audiences.

For nonprofits, visually appealing content is especially crucial as it can bring complex messages to life, make them more approachable, and foster emotional connections with audiences.

To achieve this, nonprofits must have a clear understanding of their target audience and what type of visual content resonates with them. This can encompass a range of mediums such as high-quality photos, infographics, videos, animations, and more.

By incorporating a mix of different visual forms, nonprofits can keep audiences interested in their message and enhance brand recall and impact.

It is important to recognize the distinctive storytelling approaches of different platforms, such as Twitter (280 characters), Instagram (one graphic), Facebook (photo and short post), TikTok (short-form video), YouTube (deeper content), Pinterest (useful for images), and LinkedIn (nonprofit page, blog posts, and information sharing).

The ultimate goal with using social media is to drive traffic to the nonprofit and raise awareness of its mission and causes. By creating visually engaging content, nonprofits can attain this, while also fostering a stronger community, and ultimately achieve their objectives with greater success.

A well-executed content strategy, leveraging visually appealing and shareable content, can position the nonprofit as a leader in its field, build stronger relationships with stakeholders, and increase impact in the communities served.

Creating visually appealing content through storytelling is an effective method for nonprofits to convey the impact of their work. This can be accomplished by sharing the stories of individuals who have benefited from the organization's efforts and highlighting the positive outcomes and impact on communities and relevant industries. By presenting these compelling stories in a visually engaging manner, nonprofits can foster stronger emotional connections with their audiences and encourage engagement and support for their cause.

Understanding the Target Audience

The key to successful communication and branding for nonprofits lies in comprehending the people they aim to serve and engage. A deep understanding of the target audience—including their needs, desires, pain points, and motivators—can inform effective messaging and storytelling, enabling nonprofits to form stronger relationships and achieve their goals.

For nonprofits, this understanding goes beyond basic demographics and psychographics to encompass the emotional and psychological drivers that impact behavior. By gaining insight into the hearts and minds of the target audience, nonprofits can create compelling messaging that resonates, foster a sense of community and connection, and motivate people to take action.

This section explores the process of understanding the target audience, including how to gather and analyze data and how to use that information to inform communication and branding efforts. Whether the goal is to increase engagement, build brand awareness, or mobilize supporters, a deep understanding of the target audience is a critical first step towards success.

To comprehend the target audience, a detective-like investigation is necessary. Understanding the target audience requires careful observation and analysis, which involves gathering data from multiple sources, examining patterns and trends, and connecting the dots.

The following is a list of strategies for understanding the target audience:

- **Surveys and questionnaires:** Directly ask individuals about their requirements, aspirations, and motivations through the use of surveys and questionnaires.
- **Demographic and psychographic research:** Study demographic information such as age, income, education, and location to comprehend the environment in which the audience resides.
- **Market research:** Examine market trends, consumer behaviors, and industry insights to grasp the audience's requirements and aspirations.
- **Social media listening:** Utilize social media monitoring tools to monitor discussions related to the nonprofit, its cause, and its competitors.
- **Focus groups:** Assemble a small group of individuals to converse about their perceptions and opinions on a particular subject.
- **Online analytics:** Evaluate website traffic, engagement metrics, and conversion rates to

comprehend how individuals interact with the content.

- **Customer feedback:** Obtain feedback from customers, clients, and supporters to understand their experiences and requirements.

Gathering and Analyzing Data

To effectively communicate and brand, it is crucial to have a comprehensive understanding of the target audience. This can be achieved by gathering and analyzing data from multiple sources, as discussed above. The process of connecting the dots and piecing together the puzzle of the target audience's needs, desires, and motivations is crucial for success. Surveys can provide excellent insights into the key areas.

Another way of gathering information and to fine tune and supplement the data from surveys is focus groups. Focus groups can serve as a complementary tool to surveys and questionnaires by providing additional depth and nuance to the data gathered. By facilitating interactive discussions with a diverse group of individuals, focus groups can help to validate or challenge the insights gathered through other means such as surveys, providing a more comprehensive understanding of the target audience's perspectives and experiences.

As such, focus groups can play an important role in strengthening the validity of the research and informing communication and branding efforts. By gathering a small, diverse group of individuals and engaging in facilitated discussions, nonprofits can gain insights into their audience's perspectives and opinions.

Here is a set of survey and focus group questions that nonprofits can use to get started:

- What motivated you to become involved with our organization?
- What first drew you to our organization?
- Can you describe our mission and values in your own words?
- How would you describe our mission and values to someone who has never heard of us before?

- What do you hope to achieve by being a part of our organization?
- What do you think is the most important issue facing our organization today?
- Are there any aspects of our organization that you would like to see improve?
- How do you feel about the level of communication and engagement from our organization?
- What is your favorite way to get involved and support our organization?
- What role do you see our organization playing in the community?
- How do you stay informed about our activities and events?
- How likely are you to recommend our organization to a friend or colleague?
- Is there anything else you would like to share with us about your experience with our organization?

By asking these questions and others like them, nonprofits can gain valuable insights into the perspectives and experiences of their members and stakeholders. This information can inform communication and branding efforts, help nonprofits identify areas for improvement, and build stronger relationships with their audience.

When it comes to focus groups, it's important to keep in mind that they should be structured and facilitated in a way that promotes open and respectful discussions and encourages participants to share their opinions and experiences.

Maximizing the Power of Focus Groups

Focus groups can be a potent tool for nonprofits looking to gain a deeper understanding of their target audience. By facilitating discussions among a diverse group of individuals, nonprofits can tap into a rich source of data that informs their communication and branding strategies. To make the most of focus groups, it is crucial to structure them in a way that leverages the collective wisdom of participants and encourages the sharing of candid and insightful perspectives.

The following is a step-by-step guide to structuring focus groups for maximum impact:

1. **Define objectives:** The first step in organizing a focus group is to clearly specify research objectives. By clearly stating the questions you aim to answer and the aspects of the target audience's experience you want to examine, you ensure that the focus group aligns with your goals.

2. **Select participants:** Choosing participants who represent the diversity of the target audience is crucial to gathering a diverse and representative sample of data. Consider factors such as age, gender, cultural background, and familiarity with the organization when making your selection.

3. **Foster conducive environment:** The physical setting of the focus group should be designed to facilitate open and respectful discussion. Consider factors such as lighting, seating arrangements, and the presence of recording devices to ensure participant comfort and engagement.

4. **Structure discussion guide:** A well-structured discussion guide is essential to keeping the conversation on track and obtaining the desired data. Begin by identifying the key questions to answer and then create prompts that encourage participants to share their perspectives and experiences in detail. A combination of open-ended and closed-ended questions can capture a range of perspectives and experiences.

5. **Skilled facilitation:** A focus group's success heavily relies on the facilitator's skill. The facilitator should be trained in best practices of focus group facilitation and create a safe and supportive environment for participants. They should also encourage participants to share their opinions.

6. **Analyze and utilize data:** After the focus group is complete, it is time to analyze the collected data. Look for patterns and themes in the data and consider how the insights can inform communication and branding efforts. With a clear understanding of the target audience's needs, desires, and motivations, strategies can be developed that are more

effective and impactful, ultimately supporting your mission and creating a better world.

Focus groups are an effective means for nonprofits to gain insights into their target audience. By implementing these steps and utilizing the collective knowledge of participants, valuable data can be obtained to inform communication and branding strategies, leading to greater success and impact.

Defining Brand Values and Messaging

A nonprofit's brand is more than just a logo or a tagline—it's the emotional and intangible qualities that define the organization. It's the combination of values, personality, and promise that sets it apart from the competition and helps it connect with the organization's target audience. To be successful, a brand must be authentic and reflective of the organization.

Based on the information presented up to this point, the following top ten steps can serve as a guide to creating a strong and compelling brand:

1. **Establish mission and values:** Prior to developing a robust brand, it is important to have a clear understanding of the organization's mission and values as discussed in the strategic planning section. The brand should embody these principles and serve as a constant reminder of the purpose and principles of the organization.

2. **Perform brand assessment:** Examine the existing brand materials and evaluate their efficacy. Determine what is effective, what needs improvement, and what can be adjusted. This information will play a crucial role in shaping the brand moving forward. Do all elements of the branding fit together cohesively and clearly represent the organization, or is it a hodgepodge of conflicting designs?

3. **Determine target audience:** To create a brand that resonates with the target audience, a clear understanding of their characteristics, priorities, and motivators is necessary.

Conduct research and focus groups and gather relevant data to gain insight into the target audience.

4. **Specify unique value proposition:** What distinguishes the organization from others in the same field? The unique value proposition is the key benefit offered to the target audience and what makes the organization stand out.

5. **Determine brand personality and tone:** The brand personality and tone should align with the mission and values, attract the target audience, and be consistent across all touchpoints. Choose a personality and tone that feels authentic and natural to the organization.

6. **Formulate messaging:** Construct messaging that is clear, concise, and compelling. This messaging should communicate the unique value proposition, appeal to the target audience, and reflect the brand personality and tone.

7. **Develop visual identity:** The visual identity—including the logo, colors, and imagery—should be consistent with the messaging and represent the brand personality and tone.

Choose design elements that are unique, memorable, and appealing to the target audience.

8. **Formulate content strategy:** Formulate a content strategy that encompasses blog posts, social media updates, and other forms of content aimed at communicating the brand and engaging the target audience.

9. **Evaluate and refine the brand:** Evaluate the brand and gather feedback from the target audience, stakeholders, and key partners. Use this feedback to refine the brand and make any necessary changes.

10. **Ensure consistency:** Ensuring consistency across all touchpoints is crucial to establishing a strong and impactful brand. Ensure that messaging, visual identity, and tone are consistent, and that all materials align with the mission and values.

Establishing a unique and impactful brand takes effort and a dedication to consistency. But the reward of standing out and establishing a strong connection with the target audience makes it all worth it.

Crafting a Compelling Brand Narrative

A brand narrative, or brand story, can be a powerful tool for a nonprofit seeking to establish an emotional connection with their target audience. It is a story that gives meaning and significance to the brand and helps it stand apart from competitors. A captivating brand narrative is more than a collection of facts about the organization; it is an emotional journey that creates a bond between the brand and its audience.

To create a compelling brand narrative, it's essential to understand what makes the organization unique and what sets it apart from others in the same field. This requires an in-depth examination of the mission, values, and impact to determine the core components of the brand story.

Subsequently, the target audience should be considered, including what motivates them to support the cause and what they aspire to achieve by being a part of the organization. The brand narrative should cater to these values and desires and inspire the audience to take action.

Once the brand narrative has been determined, the messaging should be crafted. The brand story should be concise, memorable, and emotionally impactful, inspiring, motivating, and connecting with the audience on a deep level.

To bring the brand story to life, consider incorporating visual and sensory elements into the messaging. Utilize storytelling techniques such as anecdotes and case studies to highlight the impact of the organization and help the audience understand the difference being made.

It's crucial to ensure that the brand story is consistently shared through all communication channels, including the website, social media, fundraising materials, and events. This helps establish a strong, recognizable brand that resonates with the target audience and supports the mission.

The following is an example of a compelling brand narrative:

charity: water

The *charity: water* organization was founded in 2006 with the goal of bringing clean and safe drinking water to people in developing countries. The founder, Scott Harrison, was inspired to start *charity: water* after a life-changing trip to Africa where he witnessed the devastating impact of the water crisis firsthand.

charity: water's brand story is built on the idea of hope and the belief that access to clean water can transform lives and communities. The organization's visual identity is simple and clean, reflecting the purity of the water they aim to provide. Their messaging is centered around the human impact of the water crisis and the transformative power of clean water.

One of *charity: water's* defining brand elements is their innovative funding model. The organization uses 100% of the public donations to fund water projects and covers overhead costs through private donations. This approach helps to build trust and credibility with donors and reinforces the organization's commitment to its mission.

Another key aspect of *charity: water's* brand story is its emphasis on transparency and accountability. The organization provides detailed information about each project it funds, including photos, GPS coordinates, and updates on progress. This level of transparency helps to build trust with donors and creates a strong emotional connection with the communities served.

Overall, *charity: water's* brand story is a powerful example of how a nonprofit can use its mission, values, and messaging to build a strong, impactful brand. By telling a compelling and authentic story, the organization has been able to connect with its target audience and secure the support needed to make a lasting impact.

As this example demonstrates, creating a compelling brand story is a critical step in establishing a powerful and impactful brand. By crafting a story that speaks to the organization's audience and reflects the unique values and impact of the organization, a strong emotional connection can be built, which can achieve greater mission impact.

Building a Consistent Brand Image

Building a consistent brand image for a nonprofit organization requires a strategic and deliberate approach. The following are some steps to consider:

- **Establishing brand values and mission:** As we noted many times earlier, to create a cohesive brand image, it is crucial to have a clear understanding of the organization's values and mission. This helps direct decision-making and ensures that branding efforts align with the purpose of the organization.

- **Creating a brand style guide:** This guide should encompass all aspects of the brand, including typography, color scheme, logo utilization, and imagery. The consistent use of these elements across all communication materials will help establish a uniform brand image.

- **Emphasizing high-quality visuals:** Investing in high-quality visuals, such as professional photography and graphics, can effectively convey the intended message and reinforce the brand image.

- **Ensuring consistent messaging:** All messaging, both written and verbal, must be consistent and align with the organization's brand values and mission.
- **Involving stakeholders:** Encourage stakeholders, including members, staff, volunteers, and supporters, to use the branding consistently and accurately. Provide resources, such as the brand style guide, to assist them.
- **Monitoring and adjusting:** Regularly assess the organization's brand image and make any necessary adjustments to maintain consistency and relevance.

Creating a consistent brand image is a vital aspect of a successful nonprofit organization. It requires a dedicated effort and commitment to ensuring that the organization's purpose and mission are effectively and consistently conveyed to its stakeholders.

Strategic Communications Planning

Developing a strategic communications plan is a fundamental step in achieving this objective. It involves the creation of a roadmap that defines the goals, target audiences, key messages, and communication channels to be used.

The plan should outline a timeline for implementation and consider how it will be integrated with the overall organizational strategic plan and evaluated and adjusted over time. This plan will provide a structured approach to effectively communicate the organization's brand to its stakeholders, ensuring consistency across all touchpoints.

The following steps are involved in the creation of a strategic communications plan:

1. **Establish objectives and goals:** Begin by defining the particular objectives and goals to achieve with the communications plan. This may include raising brand awareness, driving

increased website traffic, or boosting fundraising efforts.

2. **Conduct an analysis:** Evaluate the present state of communications and the environment in which the organization operates. Identify the strengths and weaknesses, assess the challenges, and examine the competition.

3. **Identify the target audience:** A thorough understanding of the target audience is critical in determining the most effective strategies and tactics for reaching them. Determine the audience's demographics, needs, interests, and motivations.

4. **Determine key messages:** Decide on the key messages that are to be communicated to the target audience and make sure they align with your objectives and goals.

5. **Select tactics and channels:** Based on the objectives, target audience, and key messages, choose the tactics and channels that are most likely to reach your audience. This may include social media, email marketing, website content, and events.

6. **Develop a timeline:** Create a timeline for the communications plan, including deadlines for each tactic and goal.
7. **Assess resource requirements:** Determine the budget and resources needed to execute the plan, ensuring that the necessary staff and support are available.
8. **Monitor progress and make adjustments:** Regularly review and evaluate the communications plan to determine what is working and what is not. Make necessary adjustments to improve results and achieve goals.

By following these steps, a comprehensive and effective strategic communications plan can be established which aligns with the strategic plan of the organization.

Utilizing Digital and Traditional Channels

To communicate a nonprofit's brand effectively in today's fast-paced world, it is important to utilize a blend of digital and traditional communication channels. The key is to determine the most appropriate channels for the organization and how to effectively utilize them.

The following steps can be considered when integrating digital and traditional channels into a communication strategy:

1. Assess the current environment and determine the organization's target audience.
2. Identify the objectives and goals of the communication strategy.
3. Evaluate the strengths and limitations of various digital and traditional communication channels.
4. Determine which channels will be most effective for reaching the target audience and align with the objectives and goals.
5. Create a plan that outlines the specific tactics and messages for each channel.
6. Implement the plan and regularly monitor its effectiveness.
7. Make adjustments as necessary to optimize the results of the communication strategy.

By considering these steps, a well-rounded communication strategy can be developed that maximizes impact and reaches the target audience effectively.

The utilization of effective communication channels is a crucial aspect in the dissemination of a nonprofit's brand and message to its target audience. There are several available channels, including:

- **Social media:** As mentioned previously, platforms like Facebook, Twitter, and Instagram can reach a broad audience and foster real-time engagement.
- **Email marketing:** This cost-effective method allows for targeted outreach and can be utilized to share updates, promotions, and important information.
- **Website:** A comprehensive website plays a crucial role in a nonprofit's online presence and serves as the hub for information about the organization, its purpose, and opportunities for involvement.
- **Video marketing:** Videos are a powerful tool for storytelling and connecting with viewers on

an emotional level. They can be shared via platforms such as YouTube and Vimeo to reach a wide audience.

- **Direct mail:** Direct mail tactics such as newsletters and postcards can target a specific audience and provide updates on the organization.

- **In-person events:** Hosting events, including galas, fundraisers, and volunteer opportunities, can foster engagement with supporters and raise awareness for the organization.

By utilizing a combination of digital and traditional communication channels, a nonprofit can effectively reach its target audience and build its brand.

Measuring the Effectiveness of Communication Efforts

Measuring the effectiveness of a nonprofit's brand communication efforts is critical to ensuring that resources are being used effectively to engage audiences and achieve organizational goals.

In order to accurately measure the impact of brand communication efforts, a clear understanding of the target audience, relevant key performance indicators, and communication channels is essential. This necessitates a strategic and data-driven approach that leverages both quantitative and qualitative metrics to track the effectiveness of communication initiatives.

There are many online tools that provide campaign analytics, channel management, and event-triggered actions (i.e. if there is a significant event that triggers a news article).

Effective measurement of brand communication efforts starts with setting clear and measurable goals, such as increasing brand recognition, creating engagement, or driving traffic to the website.

Once these goals have been established, it is essential to identify the key performance indicators that will help track progress towards these goals.

For example, if the goal is to increase brand recognition, it can be useful to track metrics such as the number of mentions of the nonprofit's brand on social media, the number of times the organization's brand is searched for online, or the number of impressions it receives from online ads.

Collecting qualitative data, in addition to quantitative metrics, is crucial for gaining a comprehensive understanding of audience interaction with a brand. This can be achieved through various methods, such as surveys, focus groups, or monitoring social media conversations.

The qualitative data provides valuable insight into the emotional impact the brand has on its audience and helps to identify areas that require improvement in communication efforts.

By incorporating both qualitative and quantitative metrics, organizations can create a comprehensive overview of their brand communication strategies, making informed decisions on how to optimize their efforts.

Continuously tracking the impact of these strategies over time allows organizations to continuously improve their brand communication approach, maximizing their impact and attaining their goals.

Chapter Thirteen: Trends and Challenges in Nonprofit Leadership

As the world continues to rapidly evolve and technology advances at an unprecedented pace, nonprofits must adapt and innovate to stay relevant and achieve their goals. The future of these organizations lies in embracing new and innovative strategies, leveraging technology to its fullest potential, and continuously evaluating and refining their approach to better serve their members and communities.

The trend towards greater transparency and accountability in the nonprofit sector will continue to play a significant role in shaping the future of membership associations and foundations. With the increasing availability of data and analytical tools, organizations will need to focus on demonstrating their impact and delivering measurable results in order to build trust and maintain their reputation.

In addition, the rise of digital communication and online platforms will fundamentally change the way that membership associations and foundations interact with their members and supporters. Utilizing these tools to build and strengthen relationships, engage members, and drive action will be essential to success in the years to come.

The future also holds the promise of new and innovative fundraising strategies, as well as the continued growth of social impact investing. Nonprofits will need to explore and embrace these new opportunities to diversify their revenue streams and ensure their long-term sustainability.

Ultimately, the future of nonprofits will be determined by their ability to evolve, adapt, and continuously improve. By embracing new technologies, adopting innovative strategies, and maintaining a focus on mission and impact, these organizations can ensure their continued success and effectiveness in serving their members and communities.

Top Trends and Challenges

Let's dive deeper to explore the most significant trends and challenges facing nonprofits today:

- **Demands for increased accountability and transparency:** In today's society, it is crucial for nonprofits to demonstrate their impact, efficiency, and transparency to stakeholders—including members, donors, supporters, the general public, and other key stakeholders. To meet these demands, nonprofits must implement strong accounting and reporting practices and ensure that their operations align with their mission.

- **Rise of digital and technology-driven solutions:** The rise of technology is transforming the nonprofit sector, and organizations must embrace digital solutions to remain competitive. Digital tools—such as online membership and fundraising platforms, data analytics, artificial intelligence, and social media—can help nonprofits reach new audiences, improve operations, and increase their impact.

- **Competition for funding and other resources:** Nonprofit organizations, whether they are foundations or membership associations, face intense competition for funding and other resources. To thrive, they must continually seek out new sources of funding and establish strong relationships with funders and donors. This requires an understanding of the needs and motivations of their target audience and the ability to effectively communicate their value proposition. By doing so, nonprofits can improve their chances of success and secure the resources needed to achieve their mission.

- **Increased scrutiny and regulation:** Nonprofits face increasing scrutiny from regulators, the media, and the public. Organizations must be diligent in their compliance with legal and regulatory requirements and have robust risk management policies and procedures in place.

- **The growing need for data-driven decision-making:** Data-driven decision-making is becoming increasingly important for nonprofits. Organizations must collect, analyze, and use data to make informed decisions, evaluate the impact of their programs, and continually improve their operations.

- **A shift towards collaboration and partnerships:** Nonprofits are increasingly realizing the benefits of working together, both within the sector and with other organizations. By forming partnerships, nonprofits can share resources, combine their expertise, and maximize their impact.

- **Changing demographics of members, donors and volunteers:** Nonprofits must stay adaptable in response to the ever-changing demographics of their members, donors, and volunteers to remain effective. This requires a tailored approach to fundraising, member and volunteer recruitment, and engagement strategies based on an understanding of motivations, preferences, and behaviors of different demographic groups. Staying informed of changes through ongoing research and analysis, embracing new approaches and technologies are crucial. By embracing changing demographics, nonprofits can ensure that their programs make a meaningful impact for years to come.

- **Growing focus on impact and outcomes:** Nonprofit organizations are under increasing pressure to demonstrate the impact of their work and deliver meaningful outcomes to their members, donors, and other key stakeholders. As a result, many organizations are shifting their focus to outcomes-based approaches that allow them to track their progress and measure the impact of their programs and services.

- **Emergence of new social and environmental issues:** With the increasing speed of social and environmental changes, nonprofit organizations are facing new and complex issues that require innovative and adaptive approaches. As these issues arise, it is important for nonprofits to stay informed, engage with their members, donors, and other key stakeholders, and collaborate with other organizations to find effective solutions.

- **Increased demand for evidence-based practices:** Nonprofits are increasingly being held to higher standards of accountability, which means that they must demonstrate the effectiveness of their programs and services. Evidence-based practices, which rely on data and research to inform decision-making, are becoming increasingly important in this context.

- **Balancing online and in-person engagement:** With the increasing popularity of online platforms and digital tools, nonprofits are faced with the challenge of balancing their online and in-person engagement strategies. This requires careful consideration of the strengths and limitations of each approach, and the development of a balanced and integrated approach that maximizes impact and reach.

- **Development of new funding models:** The traditional funding models for nonprofits are changing, and organizations are exploring new and innovative ways to secure funding. This may involve exploring alternative funding sources, developing new partnerships, or experimenting with new business models.

- **The need for effective talent management and leadership development:** Nonprofit organizations rely heavily on their staff, volunteers, and board members, and it is critical that these individuals are equipped with the skills, knowledge, and leadership abilities necessary to succeed. Effective talent management and leadership development programs can help organizations to build strong and sustainable teams.

- **The importance of risk management and governance:** Nonprofit organizations face a wide range of risks, from financial and operational risks, to reputational and legal risks. Effective risk management and governance practices can help organizations to mitigate these risks and maintain their focus on their mission.

- **Development of new advocacy and policy strategies:** Nonprofit organizations have long played an important role in advocating for social and environmental change, but the political landscape is constantly evolving. Organizations must be prepared to adapt their advocacy and policy strategies in response to changing conditions and to ensure that their voices are heard on the issues that matter most to them.

- **Growing importance of data privacy and security:** As nonprofits collect and manage vast amounts of sensitive information about individuals, organizations, and communities, it is becoming increasingly critical to protect this data from unauthorized access, theft, and misuse. Nonprofits must adopt robust security measures to ensure the privacy and confidentiality of their data, including data encryption, secure backups, firewalls, and access controls. Additionally, they must comply with various data privacy regulations, such as the General Data Protection Regulation (GDPR) and the California Consumer Privacy Act (CCPA).

- **Emergence of new forms of social entrepreneurship:** The traditional model of nonprofit organizations providing member-focused and/or charitable services is being disrupted by a new breed of social entrepreneurs who aim to tackle social and environmental issues by leveraging business principles and practices. These organizations blur the lines between for-profit and nonprofit and seek to generate both social impact and financial returns. Nonprofits must stay abreast of these emerging trends and embrace new models that can help them achieve their missions more effectively.

- **Importance of storytelling and branding:** Nonprofits must tell their stories in a compelling and authentic way to engage and inspire their stakeholders. They must develop a clear and compelling brand that reflects their mission and values and use this brand to differentiate themselves from other organizations. To effectively communicate their brand, nonprofits must use a mix of digital and traditional marketing channels, such as social media, email, events, and print materials.

- **Preparing for emerging trends and disruptions in the sector:** The nonprofit sector is constantly evolving, and organizations must be prepared to adapt and respond to new challenges and disruptions. This requires foresight and agility, as well as the ability to anticipate and respond to emerging trends and new technologies. Nonprofits must be proactive in seeking out new opportunities, experimenting with new ideas, and continuously learning and improving. By staying ahead of the curve, nonprofits can ensure their long-term success and impact.

Mega Issues in Nonprofits

In the nonprofit sector, mega issues can loom like dark clouds on the horizon, threatening the very existence of organizations that are dedicated to making a positive impact on society. These issues are not small, localized problems, but rather, large-scale challenges that affect the entire field or industry. Mega issues are complex and multifaceted, and they require a deep understanding of the root causes and potential solutions in order to be effectively addressed. Keep a close eye on the following mega issues, as they have the potential to significantly impact your organization.

The Membership Model Is Broken

The membership model, once the hallmark of nonprofit associations, has proven to be a thing of the past. In a rapidly changing world, the traditional membership structure simply cannot keep pace with the needs of today's organizations.

This is not to say that the membership model is completely dead, but rather that it is no longer the best option for many nonprofits.

At the heart of the problem is the fact that the membership model is based on a one-size-fits-all approach. This model assumes that all members will have the same level of commitment and involvement, and that they will all derive equal value from their membership.

However, this is simply not the case in today's society. People have different needs, different priorities, and different levels of engagement. As a result, the membership model is often unable to meet the needs of the majority of its members.

In place of the outdated membership model, nonprofits must explore new and innovative approaches. One such approach is the value-based model. This model is based on the idea that people are more likely to engage with an organization if they feel that they are receiving value in return. This can take many forms, including access to information, networking opportunities, and even tangible benefits like discounts or special events.

Another alternative is the community-based model, which is based on the idea that people are more likely to engage with an organization if they feel like they are part of a community. This model emphasizes relationship building and a sense of belonging and is particularly well-suited to organizations that are focused on creating social impact.

In exploring alternatives to traditional membership models, organizations can consider adopting a subscription or access-based approach. This model involves individuals paying for the specific resources or services they want to consume and having 24-hour access to these resources as needed. This approach allows for a more flexible and personalized experience for consumers and can help organizations ensure their long-term sustainability.

Rethinking the traditional membership model and exploring new options can help organizations continue to meet the evolving needs and preferences of their target audience.

Ultimately, the key to success for nonprofits today is to be flexible and adaptive. Organizations must be willing to experiment and try new approaches, and to continuously evaluate and refine their models based on the needs of their members and the changing landscape of the world around them.

In the end, it is not about simply replacing the membership model with something else, but rather about embracing change and evolving to meet the needs of our changing world.

In conclusion, the membership model is no longer sufficient for the needs of today's nonprofits. By embracing new and innovative models, such as the value-based and community-based models, organizations can better meet the needs of their members and create greater impact in the world.

Old-Fashioned Terminology

As we just demonstrated, gone are the days of the traditional membership model in nonprofit associations. As our world continues to evolve and change, it is crucial that the way we approach our organizations does the same. The term "association" may no longer accurately reflect the goals and objectives of these organizations, and it may be time to consider a change in nomenclature.

Imagine a world where nonprofits are not limited by the constraints of traditional labels, but instead can freely explore new and innovative approaches to their mission. By embracing a new name, nonprofits can signal to their stakeholders that they are open to change and willing to think outside the box.

For instance, imagine a nonprofit dedicated to promoting environmental sustainability that is called "The Alliance for a Greener Tomorrow". This name accurately reflects the organization's goals, but also implies a sense of community and collaboration that is central to achieving their mission.

For nonprofit organizations, reconsidering the terminology used to identify themselves can have a significant impact on their perceived value, purpose, and mission. Adopting a new name, such as an *alliance*, *partnership*, or *institute*, can modernize the image of the organization and emphasize the collaborative nature and shared responsibility of the mission.

This change in language can foster a sense of unity and purpose among members, stakeholders, and partners, while also positioning the organization as a leader in its field. A new name can signal a commitment to working together towards creating meaningful impact and can lead to new opportunities, increased membership, and overall success in advancing the mission.

In conclusion, the power of words should not be underestimated. The naming of a nonprofit can have a profound impact on how it is perceived, both internally and externally. By rethinking the labels we use, we have the power to inspire fresh perspectives and new ways of approaching our work. So, let us embrace change and rebrand our nonprofits in a way that accurately reflects the impact we aim to make in the world.

Culture That Doesn't Value Nonprofits

The perception of nonprofits has changed in recent years, and their impact and significance in the community is not always acknowledged. However, this shift in attitudes is simply a result of a cultural transformation that has placed an emphasis on individualism, entrepreneurship, and innovation.

Despite this cultural shift, the value and contribution of nonprofits in the community should not be underestimated. Nonprofits remain a vital part of our communities, providing essential services to those in need.

To overcome this perception, it is essential that nonprofits take a proactive approach to marketing and branding. They must communicate their value proposition to the public and demonstrate how their work contributes to the greater good. This can be done through the use of effective storytelling, utilizing technology to reach new audiences, and building partnerships with other organizations and businesses.

Additionally, it's important to recognize that culture and society are not static entities. They are always evolving, and nonprofits have the power to shape that evolution. By embracing innovation and finding new ways to make a positive impact, nonprofits can help to change the perception of their role in society and demonstrate their ongoing relevance and importance.

Nonprofits have an essential and irreplaceable role to play in our communities, but they must work to overcome the cultural shift that has led to a devaluation of their work. By taking a proactive approach to marketing and branding, embracing innovation, and building partnerships, nonprofits can demonstrate their value and ensure their continued success for years to come.

Innovation and Enterprise Required of Leadership

The modern nonprofit landscape is marked by an increasing need for innovation and enterprise. In order to succeed, nonprofit leaders must cultivate a culture of creativity, risk-taking, and business savvy.

This shift is driven by a number of factors, including changing public attitudes towards nonprofits, increased competition for funding and resources, and the rise of new technology and platforms that are transforming the sector.

To thrive in this rapidly evolving environment, nonprofit leaders must embrace innovation and enterprise, and cultivate the skills, mindsets, and practices that are necessary to thrive.

At the heart of this transformation is the need to break free from the traditional, reactive, and siloed approach to nonprofit leadership. Instead, nonprofit leaders must become proactive, visionary, and forward-thinking, and embrace new ways of doing business that are designed to achieve and maximize impact and create value for all stakeholders. This requires leaders to be willing to experiment, to take risks, and to embrace new models and approaches that have the potential to drive positive change.

To achieve this, nonprofit leaders must cultivate a strong entrepreneurial mindset, and be equipped with the skills and knowledge necessary to succeed in the business world. This includes a deep understanding of financial management, marketing, and fundraising, as well as a commitment to collaboration, and a willingness to partner with others to achieve common goals. Additionally, leaders must also embrace technology and innovation, and be willing to invest in tools and systems that will help their organizations to scale, automate, and streamline their operations.

Effective nonprofit leadership demands more than just a title; it requires genuine commitment and a willingness to roll up one's sleeves and do the heavy lifting. Any board member who fails to be actively engaged in the nonprofit's work must recognize that it is time to step aside and make way for someone who is capable of shouldering the workload. True leadership in the nonprofit sector entails selfless dedication to the organization's mission, not selfishly pursuing one's own interests.

Erosion

Erosion is a prevalent issue in the nonprofit sector, as the landscape is constantly changing and evolving.

Competition is increasingly moving into the space that was once solely inhabited by nonprofits, offering similar services and programs.

This shift is threatening the value of nonprofits and their ability to achieve their missions. The competition is no longer coming from just other nonprofits but from for-profit organizations and government initiatives that are capitalizing on the growing demand for social impact.

However, it's not just external competition that's causing erosion, but also the internal dynamics of the nonprofit sector. The current paradigm of fundraising and donor engagement is facing significant challenges as the market becomes more crowded and donor expectations evolve. As a result, nonprofits must adapt and innovate to maintain their relevance and impact.

The truth is, nonprofits can no longer rely on the traditional models and tactics of the past. They must embrace innovation and enterprise and see themselves as businesses with a social purpose. This means being agile, creative, and continuously seeking new and innovative ways to engage with their members, donors, and other key stakeholders and achieve their goals. Nonprofit leaders must embrace change and be willing to experiment, taking calculated risks to stay ahead of the competition and maintain their value.

As Bob Harris—CAE of Harris Management, LLC—points out, nonprofits must embrace a forward-thinking and results-oriented approach to fulfill their potential and achieve their goals. Specifically, he says, "The most successful associations don't behave like an association. It is *not* a club but rather a business with a special exemption from Federal income tax."

This important points advocates for embracing the most effective and efficient methods of operation, engaging with stakeholders and the broader community, and continually evolving to meet new and emerging challenges. By doing so, nonprofits can remain at the forefront of change and continue to drive positive impact in our world.

It's time for nonprofits, both foundations and membership associations, to step up and address the emerging issues that threaten their very existence. The status quo is no longer sufficient, and the future of these organizations depends on their ability to adapt and innovate.

The stakes are high, but so are the rewards. By embracing change, nonprofits can not only survive, but thrive, making a greater impact on the communities, professions, and industries they serve.

It's time to take action and secure the future of these vital organizations. Let's work together to ensure that the spirit of giving and service that drives nonprofits continues to flourish for generations to come.

Bonus Short Story

Muffin Mayhem: When Boards Lose Sight of the Big Picture

The board of directors was in the middle of discussing their last large event when the conversation suddenly took an unexpected turn. They were evaluating member satisfaction, exhibitor traffic, and other high-level topics, but then someone brought up the food tables.

"We had hundreds of blueberry muffins left," one board member said, "and hardly anyone touched the chocolate or plain ones. What a waste of money!"

The CEO, who was sitting in on the meeting, was quick to defend the catering company they had hired. "They provided a variety of options, but we can't control what people choose to eat."

But the board wasn't satisfied. They wanted to know exactly how much those blueberry muffins cost. When the CEO revealed that they were $50 each, the room erupted in gasps and murmurs.

The board started doing the math, trying to figure out how much money had been wasted on uneaten muffins. They were getting bogged down in the details, and it seemed like they were never going to get back to the high-level discussion they had started with, which was how to make their next event an even greater success.

Just when things were starting to feel hopeless, the board president leaned over to the treasurer and whispered something in his ear. For a moment, it looked like they were going to get back on track.

But then the president spoke up. "You know what we should do? We should have the CEO drive around and buy coffee and muffins from different stores. We'll save money and make sure we have exactly what people want!"

The room fell silent. Everyone was stunned by the president's suggestion. The CEO tried to speak up again, but the board was already deep in discussion about which stores had the best coffee and the freshest muffins. They were completely focused on the details, completely missing the big picture.

As the conversation continued to spiral into a muffin-filled abyss, the board's treasurer nervously shifted in his seat, realizing that they were missing the point of the meeting entirely. He spoke up, saying, "I understand we're all hungry, but let's not lose sight of the bigger picture here. We're discussing the success of our conference, and the number of blueberry muffins we serve won't make or break it."

His words seemed to bring the board members back to reality. They realized that they were wasting valuable time and energy on trivial details, and that their focus should be on more strategic matters.

The board president then suggested that they use this experience as a lesson in how to elevate their discussions to a more strategic level. She encouraged the board to set clear goals and objectives, establish metrics to measure success, and develop a plan of action to achieve those goals. She also said that every board member should read **The Essential Handbook for Nonprofit Leaders.**

From that day forward, the board made a conscious effort to keep their discussions focused on the big picture. They began to see real progress in their decision-making and were able to make more strategic and effective decisions for their organization.

The "Muffin Management" incident had taught them a valuable lesson in the importance of staying focused on their mission and goals, and not getting bogged down in the details.

In the end, the next conference was an even greater success, with high levels of member satisfaction and strong exhibitor traffic. The board members realized that by keeping their discussions at a strategic level and staying focused on their goals, they were able to make a real difference for their organization.

This was a classic case of "Muffin Management," where the board gets so caught up in the small details that they lose sight of the strategic goals. It's important to stay focused on the big picture and elevate discussions to a more strategic level, or else the organization will never move forward. Also, other than bruised board egos, no muffins were harmed in the development of this short story.

Thank You

This book has explored the complex and multifaceted landscape of nonprofits, and we hope that it has provided insights and inspiration to help organizations navigate this challenging yet rewarding field.

Thank you for your service and for reading **The Essential Handbook for Nonprofit Leaders**. If you found this book helpful, we would greatly appreciate it if you could take a moment to leave a review on the platform where you purchased it. Your valuable feedback can help other readers discover this book and benefit from its insights. Additionally, you can stay up-to-date with our latest book releases and access free resources by visiting our website through the QR code provided below. Thank you for your support!

About the Author

William Pawlucy, CAE, MPA, IOM
President, Association Options LLC

Introducing William Pawlucy, CAE, accomplished author and founder of Association Options LLC, a global consulting firm providing top-tier management consulting services to companies and nonprofit associations worldwide. With over 30 years of experience in various industries and extensive international exposure across the globe, Bill's unique perspective and innovative approach to management consulting make him a sought-after advisor for organizations looking to thrive.

As the author of **The Essential Handbook for Nonprofit Leaders**, Bill's expertise in nonprofit leadership is unparalleled, and his contributions have been invaluable to the industry. His extensive consulting experience, combined with his authorship, has provided him with an unparalleled insight into the challenges and opportunities facing organizations today. When he's not working, he enjoys spending quality time with his family and pets.

Discover more about Bill's work and Association Options at www.AssociationOptions.com.

Made in the USA
Middletown, DE
16 October 2023

40935190R00194